RECIPES FROM AN
INDIAN
KITCHEN

RECIPES FROM AN
INDIAN
KITCHEN

AUTHENTIC RECIPES FROM ACROSS INDIA

This edition published by Parragon Books Ltd in 2013
LOVE FOOD is an imprint of Parragon Books Ltd

Parragon Books Ltd
Chartist House
15–17 Trim Street
Bath BAI IHA, UK
www.parragon.com / lovefood

ISBN 978-1-4723-2695-9

Printed in China

New recipes by Sunil Vijayakar
Introduction by Manju Malhi
Recipe photography by Mike Cooper
Home economy by Lincoln Jefferson
Designed by Geoff Borin

Notes for the Reader
This book uses both metric and imperial measurements. Follow the same units of measurement throughout; do not mix metric and imperial. All spoon measurements are level: teaspoons are assumed to be 5 ml, and tablespoons are assumed to be 15 ml. Unless otherwise stated, milk is assumed to be full fat, eggs and individual vegetables are medium, and pepper is freshly ground black pepper. Unless otherwise stated, all root vegetables should be washed in plain water and peeled prior to using.

For best results, use a food thermometer when cooking meat and poultry – check the latest government guidelines for current advice.

Garnishes, decorations and serving suggestions are all optional and not necessarily included in the recipe ingredients or method.

The times given are an approximate guide only. Preparation times differ according to the techniques used by different people and the cooking times may also vary from those given. Optional ingredients, variations or serving suggestions have not been included in the time calculations.

Recipes using raw or very lightly cooked eggs should be avoided by infants, the elderly, pregnant women, convalescents and anyone suffering from an illness. Pregnant and breastfeeding women are advised to avoid eating peanuts and peanut products. Sufferers from nut allergies should be aware that some of the ready-made ingredients used in the recipes in this book may contain nuts. Always check the packaging before use.

Vegetarians should be aware that some of the ready-made ingredients used in the recipes in this book may contain animal products. Always check the packaging before use.

Picture acknowledgements
The publisher would like to thank Getty Images Ltd for permission to reproduce copyright material on the following pages:
2, 6, 10–11, 12 (t), 13 (b), 14 (t), 15 (b), 16, 18–19, 24–25, 30 (t, cl & cr), 31, 38–39 (all), 52 (t & b), 53, 60–61, 74–75 (all), 90 (t, bl & br), 91, 98–99, 122, 123, 142–143, 150 (t & b), 151, 164–165, 174 (tl, tr & b), 175, 186–187, 198 (tl, tr & b), 199 & 210–211.

CONTENTS

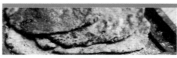

INTRODUCTION

The Indian kitchen is not only the focal point for cooking but also the essential hub of the home where family members can come together. It has long been the Indian woman's domain – responsible for keeping it pristine and in working order, she has taken pride of place in the one room where her rules have reigned for decades.

Traditionally her day would begin early. She would bathe before entering the kitchen because this room would be considered sacred. She would offer a prayer to the gods and light incense, whose heady fragrance would suffuse the fresh morning air. The water would be boiling in a stainless steel vessel on a customary Indian stove (chulha). She would take out a box of tea leaves, which she would store in her Aladdin's cave of ingredients along with an array of spices, pickles, nuts, rice and flours. Then the preparation of the first meal of the day would begin. It could be an assortment of dishes – ranging from freshly cooked breads and pancakes to eggs and Indian sweetmeats – for the family to eat at home or to be packed up ready to go when they head off out, either to school or work. The menus for the meals for the rest of the day would have already been planned in advance, depending on the availability of seasonal ingredients. All meals in India are given equal importance and lunch is served

with as much attention to detail and effort as supper time and tea time, which then see another elaborate spread of sweet and savoury snacks and appetizers (namkeen). However, the most engaging meal of the day would have to be dinner time, quite late in the day, when the family would share their day's experiences and catch up on news. The dinner setting could consist of two or three vegetable dishes along with freshly made chapattis and rice. Just before bedtime, hot milk flavoured with sugar and often cardamom would be drunk, not only by the children but also by the adults of the house.

In modern India, the role of the kitchen has changed dramatically to suit the needs of a dynamic lifestyle in a fast-paced society. The urban areas of the world's largest democracy find professional men and women skipping many traditional practices, including breakfast, to save time and to meet the demands of their jobs. This has created a new style of eating, be it in the home or outside, and has evolved into innovative meals.

BRIEF HISTORY OF
INDIAN CUISINE

The Indian food we know today is steeped in a rich culinary history. It is regarded by many that the origins of Indian history and civilization are as old as mankind itself and evidence of one of the earliest civilizations in the world, known as the Harappan civilization, dating back to around 2500BC, can be found at a site called Mohenjodaro in southern Pakistan, formerly part of India. Animal bones found at Mohenjodaro indicate that meat was eaten. Settlers started to farm, which led to the discovery of grains, such as wheat and barley. Pulses and rice also became a staple food in their diet. Ancient tandoor ovens have been found at the archaeological site, meaning that baking was popular. Also found was proof of objects that could only have come from the Middle East region, indicating the first movement of outsiders into the country with extensive trade both by land and sea to the Indus Valley cities, where there was an exchange of foods, seeds and plants, becoming one of the first external influences. This was called the Indus Valley Civilization.

Life appeared to be ordered until around 1600BC when it begun to decline and a new wave of people, known as Aryans, from Central Asia entered India. They were a semi-nomadic race who wandered with herds of cattle. Gradually they evolved into a more settled society and it is thought that around 1000BC the roots of Hinduism were shaped. This led to the development of the Hindu caste system dividing food habits of people by caste. And among this rigid tier system of classes, determined by heredity, the Brahmins or priests at the top were vegetarians, while the Kshatriyas or warriors ate meat. Half a century later, around the time of the birth of Lord Buddha, a new religion or philosophy of Buddhism began to be practised and Jainism was also emerging. The latter had a marked influence on the cuisine. Jains are strong believers in non-violence and their food, apart from being cooked without meat, is also cooked without onions and garlic or any other root vegetable that might kill insects or other animals living in the soil.

By far the biggest external influence on Indian cuisine would have to be the religious faith of Islam. From about 700AD, India was invaded by Arab Muslims and, for the next two centuries, a magnificent superpower of that period, commonly known as the Mughal Empire, was established. At the turn of the thirteenth century, they made India their home and remained at the helm of power for over 500 years up until the early 1800s. Mughal culture had a lasting impact on the cuisine of India, thus shaping and changing the face of Indian gastronomy. It is the kind of cuisine that people now tend to associate with India. The rulers saw food as an artform with recipes containing as many as twenty-five spices delicately cooked and blended, yet each dish by itself was just a small part of an opulent, lavish feast with endless courses. The Mughal empire introduced rosewater, nuts, dried fruits, saffron, dairy products (milk, cream, butter and yogurt) and the dum style of cooking dishes in a sealed vessel. One of the Mughal dynasties to invade India was the Sultan dynasty in Hyderabad in southern India where these culinary influences emanated into the regions culminating in extravagant rice dishes (biryanis).

India can be one of the few countries in the world where people of all religions celebrate all festivals and their culinary traditions – for example, Muslims celebrate Diwali (the Hindu festival of light) while Christians take part in Eid. The majority of festivals observed in India are associated with specific regional cuisines. Although India is famed for its curries, most festivals revolve around the unifying love of sugary treats and almost everyone is allowed to forget their culinary inhibitions and enjoy sweets to the fullest. Many of the desserts are prepared with nuts, rice, lentils, wheat, sugar, cardamom and saffron. The largest festival in India is Diwali, around October–November, when many recipes found in Mughal cooking are adopted to make elaborate feasts.

The cuisine of Goa in western India is influenced by Portuguese style of cooking using European ingredients. The Portuguese, led by Vasco da Gama, started the eventual colonization of India in the fifteenth century, only to be overtaken by the British who ruled the subcontinent from the eighteenth century onwards. It would be fair to say that the British love affair with 'curry' blossomed and resulted in, amongst other things, the emergence of Anglo-Indian cuisine and typical Raj traditions, such as high tea. When British rule over India ended in 1947, the subcontinent was divided into two countries – India and Pakistan, which at the time included part of what later would become Bangladesh. The resulting movement of people within the subcontinent and consequently the migration of various regional cultures to Europe, Asia and the Americas meant that their distinct cooking styles inevitably merged, resulting in today's Indian cuisine ranging from Mughlai (Mughal cuisine) to Anglo-Indian to modern Chinese- influenced Indian food.

Many Indian dishes may have evolved from the principles of Ayurveda – a holistic approach to food and its preparation based around balancing the six tastes of sweet, sour, salty, pungent, bitter and astringent.

REGIONAL CUISINE

NORTH

Lamayuru monastery at sunrise, Jammu and Kashmir

Around the world, many menus of Indian restaurants include dishes from the north of India. The north is the home of the tandoor and tandoori cooking, where food is cooked in a clay oven at extremely high temperatures. People of the north have hearty appetites and love to indulge. The curries are predominantly thick, rich and often have creamy sauces and they are served with breads. With the northern states of Punjab and Haryana considered India's bread basket, rotis, parathas (flaky bread), naans (tandoor-baked leavened bread) and other wheat-based preparations are more popular than rice. However, the Himalayas are close to Jammu and Kashmir and provide the water to grow the basmati rice that is exported abroad. With very hot summers and severely cold winters, the north of India grows a wide mixture of fruits and vegetables, such as apples from the state of Himachal Pradesh; cauliflower from Madhya Pradesh; as well as okra, mustard and spinach greens. The Indian state of Punjab is known for its rich dishes using dairy products, such as ghee (clarified butter), paneer (Indian cheese), milk and cream, and nuts and dried fruits. Meat dishes reflect Mughal and Kashmiri styles of cuisine with the creation of rich

pilaus and biryanis. Notable popular dishes from the north of India include mattar paneer (peas and cheese), chicken tikka, butter chicken, fish Amitsari, meat kebabs, samosas and dal makhani (buttery lentils) made predominantly using cumin, coriander, dried red chillies, cardamom, cinnamon, cloves and the spice blend garam masala. Dishes are cooked in vegetable and groundnut oil, with ghee being used on special occasions.

Spiced gram flour flatbreads (besan ki roti), p193

The south of India has a hot and humid climate and its states are surrounded by three bodies of water – the Arabian Sea on the west, the Bay of Bengal on the eastern side and the Indian Ocean towards the southern side – making all the states in the south coastal. Because of its geographical location, seafood is very high on the menu. Rainfall is abundant so the supply of fresh fruit, vegetables and rice is ample. The cuisines of the states of Karnataka, Kerala, Tamil Nadu and Andhra Pradesh encompass the south. These regions are famed for their spices, such as peppercorns, cloves, cardamoms, ginger and cinnamon. In the state of Andhra Pradesh, the food is heavily influenced by the legacy of the Mughal Empire. Hyderabad, the capital of Andhra Pradesh, was ruled by the Nizams during the eighteenth century, when the food was shaped by Turkish, Arabic and Irani tastes. This culminated in dishes such as the Hyderabadi biryani (baked lamb with rice) and haleem (a ground mince and wheat savoury porridge). The state of Kerala, known as the land of coconuts, specializes in Malabari cuisine using seafood combined with fresh spices, such as curry leaves, mustard seeds, asafoetida, along with tamarind and coconut to create sumptuous fish curries. The state is also known for its vegetarian traditional banquet, known as sadya, comprising of boiled rice served with a selection of side dishes made with vegetables and lentils and a sweet preparation called payasam. Recipes from Tamil Nadu make abundant use of chillies – this style of cooking is known as Chettinad cuisine. Tamil Nadu is also celebrated for its dosas and idlis. Dosas are savoury pancakes made from a batter of fermented lentils and rice, commonly accompanied by sambhar (a spicy vegetable and lentil dish) and coconut- and chilli-based chutneys. Idlis are made from the same ingredients as dosas but are steamed instead of fried. Despite India being one of the largest tea growers in the world, south Indians are staunch coffee drinkers and Mysore coffee is their favourite 'tea' time drink.

Peppered south Indian chicken curry (murgh chettinad), p129

The Kerala backwaters

SOUTH

EAST

Of all the regions of India, the heaviest rainfall is in the east of the country so rice grown in the vast paddy fields is the staple of the people of the states of West Bengal, Orissa, Sikkim, Nagaland, Assam, Manipur, Arunachal Pradesh, Meghalaya, Mizoram and Tripura. The cuisine of these regions is strongly influenced by Chinese and Mongolian cooking styles so the preparations are simple with uncomplicated flavours and the steaming of food is preferred to frying. The people of West Bengal are known for their sweet tooth, which means that some of India's most sought-after desserts (sweetmeats created with dairy products, nuts and spices) come from Kolkata. Near the coastal regions of eastern India, fish is prepared in mustard oil and cooked with a spice blend known as panch phoran (Bengali five-spice seasoning). The five spices in panch phoran are cumin seeds, onion or nigella seeds, mustard seeds, fennel seeds and fenugreek seeds. East Indians inland favour beef and pork as their non-vegetarian fare. Sikkim and its surrounding states in the east have adopted the food culture of neighbouring countries like Tibet with the creation of thukpa (a clear noodle-based broth) and momos (steamed dumplings made with minced chicken or mutton, which have grown to be a popular street food and are served with a red chilli sauce dip).

Steamed chicken dumplings (murgh momo), p89

Vegetable noodle broth (thukpa), p92

The diets of people in the west of India are largely based on Hinduism and are predominantly vegetarian, particularly in the state of Gujarat. Their snacks, known as farsan, are legendary and include a huge selection of rice and gram flour savouries that are sold all over India. Similar to Kerala, Gujarat has its own style of thali serving ten vegetarian dishes on one platter. The food of Rajasthan includes meat dishes such as laal maas, which literally means 'red meat' – the colour red indicates the amount of chilli that would be used to prepare this recipe. There's also a dish that would be fair to say is an acquired taste called dal baati churma – a combination of lentils (dal), wheat flour dough balls (baati) and a sugar and wheat flour mixture (churma) cooked in clarified butter. The dry, arid and desert climate of Rajasthan means that there is a relatively small variety of vegetables available so preserving them as pickles (aachar) and chutneys is quite common, and lentils are cooked daily. Maharashtra is the state in which the commercial hub of Mumbai is located. Street food is synonymous with this city and pomfret, a popular flat fish with a distinctive flavour, is cooked in a variety of ways. Peanuts and coconut are widely available and used liberally in curries, relishes and sweets. Malvani and Konkan cuisines make the most of coconuts

and fish seasoned with a sour-tasting, deep-purple berry called kokum (mangosteen). Goa with its lush, green coastline makes use of fresh fish and is also influenced by the legacy left by the Portuguese in dishes such as vindaloo (a fiery curry made with garlic and vinegar) and xacuti (a thick chicken and coconut curry with dried red chillies) served with European bread rolls. Many of the flavours of Goan cuisine are rich and piquant and run through its cooked meats, such as their ready-made Goan spicy pork sausages (chouricos), which are eaten by the large Catholic community.

Goan spiced chicken (murgh xacuti), p137

WEST

Victoria or Chhatrapati Shivaji Terminus, Mumbai

EATING INDIAN-STYLE

Generally in Indian cuisine, there is only one course and all the dishes are served together, including any soups, but Indian restaurants throughout the world often divide dishes into starters, appetizers, mains and desserts in order to make an Indian meal more familiar to eating habits in the western world. What many consider as Indian starters and appetizers, such as deep-fried snacks like samosas and onion bhajis, are actually commonly served with tea in India, while desserts or sweet dishes are eaten during festivals. The traditional way of serving Indian food is on a thali, which is a large, stainless steel tray-like plate. The thali may contain small, stainless steel bowls (katoris) in which are placed various vegetable and lentil preparations, including relishes, while rice and bread (roti or pooris) are served in the centre of the thali. In the west and south of India, it is not uncommon to see food being served on glossy green banana leaves.

Traditionally there are no eating implements, such as knives or forks, and the food is eaten only with the right hand because the left hand is regarded as the hand that is used for cleaning purposes only. It is therefore essential to wash one's hands before eating. A portion of the bread or roti is torn and used as a scoop to gather and scoop up a quantity of an accompanying dish. Rice acts as a base for many Indian meals and only one dish is sampled with every mouthful of rice in order to fully appreciate the individual flavours and spice notes of every dish. Drinking beverages during an Indian meal is a fairly new phenomenon and, like the rice, the drink served needs to be quite neutral, such as water. However, many Indian meals are now served with sweet drinks like rose syrup beverages, beer or lager. And although certain tannins may affect the flavour of Indian foods, there are now wines that have been created to match the spices.

It would not make sense to use authentic Indian cookware and utensils that were used a century ago because they have been replaced by better, more efficient and practical kitchen equipment. So here is a list of items that would be worth stocking for everyday Indian cooking:

- KARAHI (Indian wok) or a large, heavy-based saucepan for frying foods

- TAWA or a flat, heavy griddle or pan for the preparation of rotis and pancakes

- ROLLING PIN for shaping rotis and other breads

- MEASURING SPOONS for accurate measurement of spices

- WEIGHING SCALES to make sure the ingredients are the right quantities for the right balance of spices

- SMALL FRYING PAN with a heavy base for dry-roasting spices in small batches

- METAL TONGS to turn breads and other hot foods

- STEAMER suitable for the preparation of south Indian dishes

- FOOD PROCESSOR to assist in chopping and blending ingredients

- PESTLE AND MORTAR for coarsely grinding spices

- SPICE GRINDER for preparing fresh spice blends

- PRESSURE COOKER for cooking dried beans and pulses that would otherwise take hours to cook.

ESSENTIAL EQUIPMENT FOR INDIAN COOKING

GLOSSARY OF INGREDIENTS

Asafoetida
This finely ground resin is known as 'the devil's dung' because its pungent, sulphurous aroma is very off-putting until it is cooked. Asafoetida is used only in small amounts and it is sold in block or powder form.

Banana leaves
South Indian food is often served on these large, glossy, dark-green leaves. The leaves can also be wrapped around food before cooking to seal in the flavours.

Basmati rice
Grown in the foothills of the Himalayas, this long-grain rice is valued around the world for its delicate fragrance and silky grains that separate during cooking. Outside of India, basmati rice is synonymous with Indian food, but more than twenty varieties of rice are grown and used within the country. Consequently, basmati is often saved for special occasions and celebrations.

Bay leaves
Bay leaves used in Indian cuisine are different from those used in the West. Asian bay leaves come from the cassis tree, whereas Western ones are obtained from sweet bay laurel. However, Western bay leaves are fine to use if you cannot obtain Asian ones.

Cardamom
Known as the 'queen of spices' (black pepper is the 'king'), green cardamom is one of the most popular flavourings in Indian cooking, used in both savoury and sweet dishes as well as in drinks. Although the whole pods are often used in recipes, they're not meant to be eaten so take care to remove them from the finished dish before serving. Black cardamom has a much heavier, pronounced flavour and is only used in savoury recipes. Ground cardamom is available, but grinding small quantities of the seeds at home will produce a better flavour.

Chilli powder
When fresh green chillies are ripe, they turn a rich red. These are dried to obtain dried red chillies. Chilli powder is made by finely grinding dried red chillies. Look out for bright red Kashmiri chilli powder, made from the chillies that grow in the northern region of Kashmir.

Chillies, fresh
Synonymous as chillies are with Indian food, they are relative newcomers to the Indian spice box, having been introduced by the Portuguese. Unfortunately, it is difficult to tell how hot a chilli is by appearance only. As a general rule, the small, thin ones are hot while the large, fleshy ones tend to be milder. Most of the heat is in the seeds and membranes so it is best to remove them if you prefer a milder flavour.

Cinnamon

One of the oldest spices, cinnamon is obtained from the rolled, dried bark of a tropical plant related to the laurel family. It has a warm flavour and is used in both savoury and sweet dishes.

Cloves

Frequently used whole or ground in Indian cooking, these dried flowerbuds have a strong, aromatic flavour that can be overpowering if used in abundance or chewed.

Coconut

Considered the 'fruit of the gods', coconuts are important in Hindu religious ceremonies, as well as to the kitchens of southern India and Goa. The creamy, white flesh and thin, cloudy coconut water are used in cooking and as snacks. Coconut milk is made by grating, blending and squeezing the juice from the coconut flesh. Different grades of thickness exist – the first extraction is thicker and the second, made from soaking the remaining blended coconut in water, is thinner. Coconut cream is richer and thicker than coconut milk with a higher ratio of coconut to water. Both are available ready-made in cans or cartons. Creamed coconut is available in pressed bars – you simply grate off the required amount and dissolve in boiling water.

Coriander

Fresh coriander leaves add a tangy, citrus flavour and a splash of vibrant green colour to many Indian dishes. The round seeds – with their sweet, mellow flavour – taste very different from the leaves of the fresh herb. They are sold as seeds or a ground powder.

Cumin

Popular with cooks in all regions of India, cumin is prized for its distinctive, strong flavour and digestive qualities. The thin, slightly elongated seeds are available in two varieties: brown and black. Each has their own distinctive flavour and one cannot be substituted for the other. Cumin is used either whole or ground.

Curry leaves

A hallmark of southern cooking, these have an assertive flavour. Fresh and dried versions are available. Dried ones can be stored in an airtight container and fresh ones can be frozen and used as and when required.

Dried mango powder [amchoor]

This is made from unripe green mangoes that are dried and ground to form a powder. It is used as a meat tenderizer, as well as in dishes that require a sour flavour.

Fennel seeds

These have a taste similar to that of anise. The seeds range in colour from bright green to pale green and tan and resemble a ridged grain of rice. Fennel seeds are used extensively in Indian cooking and are an essential ingredient in some key spice mixes (masalas), such as panch phoran. In India, fennel seeds are chewed as an after-dinner mouth freshener.

Fenugreek

A strong and aromatic herb, fenugreek is cultivated in India and Pakistan, but is native to the Mediterranean region. The fresh leaves are cooked like spinach and they are also dried and used in smaller quantities to flavour meat and poultry dishes. The small, irregular-shaped fenugreek seeds have a distinctive flavour and a powerful taste. They are also available in ground form.

Garam masala

The word garam means 'heat' and masala is an Indian term for a spice mix. The basic ingredients are cinnamon, cardamom, cloves and black pepper – a blend of spices believed to create body heat. Ground garam masala is usually added towards the end of cooking, whereas whole garam masala is added to the cooking fat at the start of cooking.

Garlic

Fresh garlic is an integral part of Asian cooking. It is always used crushed, finely chopped or made into a paste.

Ghee

Ghee is an Indian form of clarified butter. The traditional rich flavour of many Indian dishes, especially those from the northern regions, comes, at least in part, from cooking with ghee. Ghee can be heated to a high temperature without burning but its high cholesterol content means that it is slowly being replaced on an everyday basis with vegetable oils.

Ginger

Like garlic, ginger adds an authentic flavour to Indian cooking. This knobbly rhizome imparts a warm, spicy taste to a wide variety of meat, poultry, fish and vegetarian dishes. For the best flavour, buy fresh ginger with a tight, smooth skin — a wrinkled skin is an indication that the flesh is drying out.

Lentils, beans and peas

Dal is the word Indians use to describe both split dried lentils, beans and peas and the numerous dishes prepared with these ingredients. Dals are a daily feature of menus across India and provide the backbone of most vegetarian meals.

Mint

Introduced to India by the Persians, this fresh-tasting herb is particularly popular in northern India, where it garnishes rich meat and poultry dishes. Fresh mint also features in many chutneys, raitas and drinks.

Mustard oil

Mustard oil is a popular cooking oil, especially in Bengali cooking, with a strong, pungent flavour. To counter the pronounced flavour, many recipes begin by heating the oil until it is very hot and then allowing it to cool before reheating and adding other ingredients.

Mustard seeds

Tiny, round mustard seeds are used in cooking throughout India. Black and brown are the most common varieties and can be used interchangeably. They lend a nutty flavour to a dish. White mustard seeds are usually reserved for making pickles.

Nigella seeds

These tiny, black seeds are also known as black onion or kalonji seeds, although they have nothing to do with onions! Their flavour is nutty and peppery. They are used whole for flavouring vegetables, pickles, breads and snacks.

Palm sugar

This dark, coarse and unrefined sugar, sometimes referred to as jaggery, is made from the sap of the coconut palm tree. It usually comes in the form of a solid cake in a cone or barrel shape.

Panch phoran

Panch phoran is a Bengali spice mixture made up of equal quantities of fenugreek seeds, fennel seeds, mustard seeds, nigella seeds and cumin seeds.

Paneer

For India's millions of vegetarians, this firm, white cheese is a source of daily protein. Although paneer has a bland flavour, it readily absorbs flavours when cooked with other ingredients and its firm texture means that it is ideal for grilling and roasting. Fresh paneer is sold in Asian grocery stores, but it is simple to make at home (see recipe on page 28).

Peppercorns

Fresh green berries are dried in the sun to obtain black pepper. Green berries come from the pepper vine native to the monsoon forests of southwest India. Black peppercorns will keep well in an airtight jar, but ground black pepper loses its wonderful aromatic flavour very quickly — it is best to grind peppercorns as needed.

Poppy seeds

The opium poppy, grown mainly in the tropics, produces the best poppy seeds. There are two varieties: white and black. The white seeds are ground and added to dishes to give them a nutty flavour. They are also used as a thickener and as a topping for naan bread.

Rosewater

Rosewater is the diluted extract of a special strain of edible rose, the petals of which are often used to garnish Mughal dishes. Rose syrup, used in drinks and desserts, is made from rosewater, sugar and water.

Saffron

The most expensive spice in the world, these thin threads come from the dried stamens of the crocus flower. It is so costly because the stamens are hand-picked and around 250,000 stamens are needed to produce just 450 g/1 lb of saffron! Indian saffron is grown in Kashmir and is used to add a brilliant gold colour and a distinctive, slightly musky taste to many Indian dishes.

Silver foil [varak]

Indian desserts and sweets are elevated to special status with a decoration of edible silver (or gold) dust pressed onto delicate, ultra-thin sheets.

Tamarind

Resembling pea pods at first, tamarind turns dark brown with a thin, hard outer shell when ripe. The flesh is sold dried and has to be soaked in hot water to yield a pulp. Alternatively, ready-to-use tamarind paste is available. Valued for its distinctive and pronounced sour flavour, tamarind is added to many fish and vegetable dishes.

Turmeric

The instant sunshine of many Indian dishes, fresh turmeric rhizomes resemble fresh ginger and have a beige-brown skin and bright-yellow flesh. Fresh turmeric is dried and ground to produce this essential spice, which should be used in carefully measured quantities to prevent a bitter taste.

Yogurt

There are countless uses for yogurt in the Indian kitchen. It is used as a meat tenderizer and a souring agent, as well as being the main ingredient in numerous raitas and some chutneys. Indian yogurt, often referred to as 'curd', is made from buffalo milk. Set natural yogurt, whisked until smooth, is a good substitute.

GINGER PASTE

1 large root of fresh ginger

vegetable oil, as needed

1 Use a potato peeler to peel the ginger or scrape off the skin with a small, sharp knife.

2 Coarsely chop the ginger and put it in a blender or food processor and blend to a purée, adding enough vegetable oil to enable the blades to move. Transfer to an airtight container and store in the refrigerator for 6–8 weeks or freeze in small quantities and defrost as required.

GARLIC PASTE

6 large garlic bulbs

vegetable oil, as needed

1 Peel the garlic cloves — the easiest way to do this is to crush them lightly with the flat of the blade of a large knife — and discard the skins.

2 Put the garlic cloves in a blender or food processor and blend to a purée, adding enough vegetable oil to enable the blades to move. Transfer to an airtight container and store in the refrigerator for 6–8 weeks or freeze in small quantities and defrost as required.

GREEN CHILLI PASTE

handful of fresh green chillies

vegetable oil, as needed

1 Wash and pat dry the green chillies. Trim off the stalks and roughly chop the flesh, leaving in the seeds if wished.

2 Transfer to a blender or food processor and blend to a purée, adding enough vegetable oil to enable the blades to move. Transfer to an airtight container and store in the refrigerator for 6–8 weeks or freeze in small quantities and defrost as required.

GHEE

250 g/9 oz butter

1 Melt the butter in a large, heavy-based saucepan over a medium heat and continue simmering until a thick foam appears on the surface of the butter.

2 Simmer, uncovered, for 15–20 minutes, or until the foam separates, the milk solids settle on the bottom and the liquid becomes clear and golden. Watch closely because the milk solids at the bottom of the pan can burn quickly.

3 Meanwhile, line a sieve with a piece of muslin and place the sieve over a bowl. Slowly pour the liquid through the muslin, without disturbing the milk solids at the bottom of the pan. Discard the milk solids.

4 Leave the ghee to cool, then transfer to a smaller container, cover and chill. Store in the refrigerator for up to 4 weeks.

GARAM MASALA

2 bay leaves, crumbled

2 cinnamon sticks, broken in half

seeds from 8 green cardamom pods

2 tbsp cumin seeds

1½ tbsp coriander seeds

1½ tbsp black peppercorns

1 tsp cloves

¼ tsp ground cloves

1 Heat a dry frying pan over a high heat until a splash of water 'dances' when it hits the surface. Reduce the heat to medium, add the bay leaves, cinnamon sticks, cardamom seeds, cumin seeds, coriander seeds, peppercorns and whole cloves and dry-fry, stirring constantly, until the cumin seeds look dark golden brown and you can smell the aromas. Immediately tip the spices out of the pan and leave to cool.

2 Use a spice grinder or pestle and mortar to grind the spices to a fine powder. Stir in the ground cloves. Store in an airtight container for up to 2 months.

PANEER

2.2 litres / 4 pints milk

6 tbsp lemon juice

1 Pour the milk into a large, heavy-based saucepan over a high heat and bring to the boil. Remove the pan from the heat and stir in the lemon juice. Return the pan to the heat and continue boiling for a further minute, until the curds and whey separate and the liquid is clear.

2 Remove the pan from the heat and set aside for an hour or so, until the milk is completely cool. Meanwhile, line a sieve with a piece of muslin large enough to hang over the edge and place the sieve over a bowl.

3 Pour the cold curds and whey into the muslin, then gather up the edges and squeeze out all the excess moisture.

4 Use a piece of string to tightly tie the muslin around the curds in a ball. Put the ball in a bowl and place a plate on top. Place a food can on the plate to weigh down the curds, then chill for at least 12 hours. The curds will press into a compact mass that can be cut. Store in the refrigerator for up to 3 days.

PAO BHAJI MASALA

2 tbsp coriander seeds

1 tbsp cumin seeds

1 tsp fennel seeds

1 star anise

4 dried red chillies

6 cloves

¼ tsp cardamom seeds

1 cinnamon stick

1 tsp ground turmeric

1 tbsp dried mango powder

1 tbsp garam masala

1 tsp ground ginger

1 Heat a non-stick frying pan over a medium heat. Gently roast the coriander seeds, cumin seeds, fennel seeds, star anise, dried red chillies, cloves, cardamom seeds and cinnamon stick until they turn slightly darker and begin to release their aroma. Remove from the heat and allow to cool.

2 Use a spice grinder or pestle and mortar to grind all the whole spices to a fine powder. Stir in the remaining ingredients. Store in an airtight container for up to 2 months.

TANDOORI MASALA

2 tsp garlic powder

2 tsp ground ginger

1 tsp ground cloves

1 tsp ground cardamom seeds

1 tsp ground fenugreek

1 tsp ground cinnamon

1 tsp pepper

¼ tsp ground nutmeg

1 tbsp ground cumin

1 tbsp cayenne pepper or chilli powder

2 tbsp ground coriander

1 Place all the ingredients in a bowl and stir to mix well. Store in an airtight container for up to 2 months.

SAMBHAR MASALA

3 dried red chillies, stems removed

2 tbsp coriander seeds

2 tsp cumin seeds

2 tsp black mustard seeds

1 tsp black peppercorns

1 tsp fenugreek seeds

3 cloves

¼ tsp ground turmeric

½ tsp asafoetida

1½ tsp vegetable or groundnut oil

1½ tbsp split yellow lentils (chana dal)

1 tbsp dry unsweetened coconut

1½ tbsp split black lentils (urad dal chilke)

1 Heat a large, heavy-based saucepan over a medium–high heat. Add the dried red chillies, coriander seeds, cumin seeds, black mustard seeds, peppercorns, fenugreek seeds and cloves and dry-fry, stirring constantly, until the mustard seeds start to pop, you can smell the aromas and the seeds darken in colour but do not burn. Stir in the turmeric and asafoetida, then immediately tip the spices into a bowl.

2 Return the pan to the heat. Add the oil and heat, then stir in the split yellow lentils, coconut and split black lentils and cook for about 1 minute, until they darken in colour. Tip them out of the pan and add to the spices. Leave the mixture to cool completely.

3 Use a spice grinder or pestle and mortar to grind to a fine powder. Store in an airtight container for up to 2 months.

CHAPTER 1
RAITAS, CHUTNEYS & PICKLES

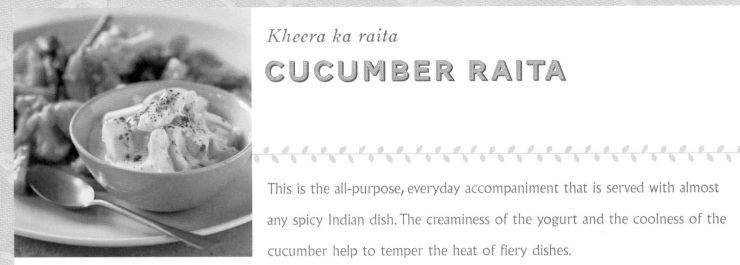

Kheera ka raita

CUCUMBER RAITA

This is the all-purpose, everyday accompaniment that is served with almost any spicy Indian dish. The creaminess of the yogurt and the coolness of the cucumber help to temper the heat of fiery dishes.

SERVES: 4

PREP: 15 minutes

COOK: 1–2 minutes, plus cooling time

1 small cucumber

175 g/6 oz wholemilk natural yogurt

¼ tsp sugar

¼ tsp salt

1 tsp cumin seeds

10–12 black peppercorns

¼ tsp paprika

1 Peel the cucumber and scoop out the seeds. Cut the flesh into bite-sized pieces and set aside.

2 Put the yogurt in a bowl and beat with a fork until smooth. Add the sugar and salt and mix well.

3 Preheat a small, heavy-based saucepan over a medium–high heat. When the pan is hot, turn off the heat and add the cumin seeds and peppercorns. Stir around for 40–50 seconds, until they release their aroma. Remove from the pan and leave to cool for 5 minutes, then crush in a mortar with a pestle.

4 Reserve ¼ teaspoon of this mixture and stir the remainder into the yogurt. Add the cucumber and stir to mix.

5 Transfer the raita to a serving dish and sprinkle with the reserved toasted spices and the paprika.

TIP

For a flavour variation, try adding a little lemon rind and juice, or stirring in some chopped fresh mint just before serving.

Aam aur annanas raita

MANGO & PINEAPPLE RAITA

Yogurt, or 'curd', as it is known in India, is a staple throughout the regions. It is eaten plain or in raitas with vegetables and fruit added. This cooling yogurt salad includes juicy diced pineapple and mango.

SERVES: 4   **PREP:** 10–15 minutes   **COOK:** 1–2 minutes

250 g/9 oz set natural yogurt

1 onion, finely sliced

1 tomato, finely chopped

1 fresh green chilli, finely chopped

100 g/3½ oz pineapple flesh, finely diced

100 g/3½ oz ripe mango flesh, finely diced

¼ tsp salt

2 tbsp vegetable or groundnut oil

1 tsp black mustard seeds

4 fresh curry leaves

1 Place the yogurt in a bowl and whisk until smooth.

2 Add the onion, tomato, chilli, pineapple, mango and salt to the yogurt and stir to mix well.

3 Heat the oil in a small frying pan, then add the mustard seeds and curry leaves. Cook, stirring constantly, for a few seconds, or until the mustard seeds start to pop.

4 Remove the pan from the heat and pour the contents over the yogurt mixture. Stir gently to mix and serve immediately or chill until required.

TIP

This raita can be stored, covered, in the refrigerator and used within 2 days.

Anaar ka raita

SOUTH INDIAN YOGURT, POMEGRANATE & PEANUT RAITA

Also known as a *pachadi* in south India, this cooling accompaniment is made more often than not with yogurt, sautéed spices and freshly grated coconut. A pachadi accompanies the main meal and is one of the dishes that makes up the *sadya* or south Indian vegetarian platter.

SERVES: 4

PREP: 10 minutes

COOK: 4–5 minutes

2 tbsp vegetable or groundnut oil

4 shallots, finely chopped

2 fresh green chillies, finely chopped

2 tsp finely grated fresh ginger

1 tsp black mustard seeds

4 fresh curry leaves

2 whole dried red chillies, broken in half

2 tsp cumin seeds

225 g/8 oz set natural yogurt, whisked

1 tsp salt

4 tbsp freshly grated coconut

2 tbsp finely chopped fresh coriander

2 tbsp pomegranate seeds

2 tbsp roughly chopped toasted peanuts

1 Heat the oil in a frying pan, add the shallots and stir-fry over a low heat for 3–4 minutes.

2 Add the green chillies, ginger, mustard seeds, curry leaves, dried red chillies and cumin seeds. Stir-fry for 1 minute, then remove from the heat.

3 Stir in the yogurt, salt, coconut and coriander. Stir to mix well and transfer to a serving bowl. Scatter over the pomegranate seeds and peanuts just before serving.

Bhindi ka raita

CRISPY OKRA RAITA

This delightful raita, from the western shores of India, is thick and cooling on the palate when served with a hot curry or spicy fried fish and rice. The crisp okra provides texture to this slightly sweet and gently spiced dish.

SERVES: 4

PREP: 10 minutes

COOK: 5–6 minutes

6 tbsp vegetable or groundnut oil

200 g/7 oz okra, trimmed and cut into 1-cm/½-inch slices

400 g/14 oz set natural yogurt

1 tsp salt

1 tsp sugar

1 tsp cayenne pepper

¼ tsp ground turmeric

1 tsp black mustard seeds

2 tbsp finely chopped fresh coriander

1 Heat 5 tablespoons of the oil in a large frying pan over a medium heat. When the oil is very hot, add the okra, toss and cook, stirring occasionally, for 3–4 minutes – the okra will slowly turn crisp and brown. Once the okra is well browned, transfer to kitchen paper and set aside until ready to serve.

2 Whisk the yogurt with the salt and sugar in a medium-sized serving bowl. Sprinkle the cayenne pepper and turmeric over the yogurt mixture, but do not mix it in.

3 Heat the remaining oil in a small frying pan over a high heat. When the oil begins to smoke, add the mustard seeds. When the mustard seeds stop popping, pour the hot oil directly on top of the cayenne pepper and turmeric. (This will cook the spices without burning them.)

4 Just before serving, place the crisp okra on top and scatter over the chopped coriander.

TIP

If you spread out the sliced okra on a baking sheet for a couple of hours to dry, it will result in a nice crispy texture when fried.

Hare dhaniye ki chutney

CORIANDER CHUTNEY

This is an example of one of the uncooked, fresh-tasting chutneys that are served throughout the day in Kerala, starting with breakfast. The bright green coriander, fresh coconut and chilli capture the flavours of the region.

SERVES: 4

PREP: 5–10 minutes

COOK: 0 minutes

1½ tbsp lemon juice

1½ tbsp cold water

85 g/3 oz fresh coriander leaves and stems, roughly chopped

2 tbsp chopped fresh coconut

1 small shallot, very finely chopped

5-mm/¼-inch piece fresh ginger, chopped

1 fresh green chilli, deseeded and chopped

½ tsp sugar, or to taste

½ tsp salt, or to taste

pinch of pepper, or to taste

1 Put the lemon juice and water in a small food processor, add half the coriander and process until it is blended and a slushy paste forms. Gradually add the remaining coriander and process until it is all blended, scraping down the sides of the processor, if necessary. If you don't have a processor that will cope with this small quantity, use a pestle and mortar, adding the coriander in small amounts.

2 Add the remaining ingredients and continue processing until they are all finely chopped and blended. Taste and adjust the seasoning, adding extra sugar and salt if needed. Transfer to a non-metallic bowl and serve immediately or cover and chill until required.

TIP

For a cooling coriander raita, stir 300 g/10½ oz wholemilk natural yogurt into the chutney and chill for at least 1 hour.

Mirch aur pyaaz ki chutney

CHILLI & ONION CHUTNEY

For those who really like hot and spicy food, this fresh chutney packs quite a punch. Gujarati people will include the chilli seeds and serve this at all meals, eating it in the summer as a snack with poppadoms or pooris.

SERVES: 4

PREP: 5–10 minutes, plus standing & chilling time

COOK: 0 minutes

1–2 fresh green chillies, finely chopped (deseeded if you like)

1 small fresh bird's eye chilli, finely chopped (deseeded if you like)

1 tbsp white wine vinegar or cider vinegar

2 onions, finely chopped

2 tbsp lemon juice

1 tbsp sugar

3 tbsp chopped fresh coriander, mint or parsley, or a combination of herbs

salt

chilli flower, to garnish (see TIP)

1 Put the chillies in a small, non-metallic bowl with the vinegar, stir around and then drain. Return the chillies to the bowl and stir in the onions, lemon juice, sugar and herbs, then add salt to taste.

2 Leave to stand at room temperature or cover and chill for 15 minutes. Garnish with the chilli flower before serving.

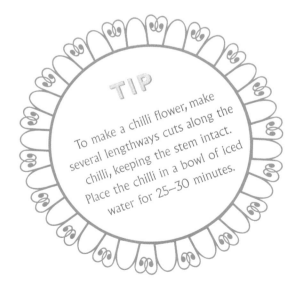

TIP

To make a chilli flower, make several lengthways cuts along the chilli, keeping the stem intact. Place the chilli in a bowl of iced water for 25–30 minutes.

Imli ki chutney

TAMARIND CHUTNEY

There isn't any mistaking the fresh, sour taste of tamarind — it adds a distinctive flavour to many dishes, especially those from southern India. More like a sauce than a thick chutney, this sweet and sour mixture is essential for serving with samosas.

SERVES: 4–6

PREP: 5–10 minutes

COOK: 35–40 minutes, plus cooling time

100 g/3½ oz tamarind pulp, chopped

450 ml/16 fl oz cold water

½ fresh bird's eye chilli, or to taste, deseeded and chopped

55 g/2 oz soft light brown sugar, or to taste

½ tsp salt, or to taste

1 Put the tamarind and water in a heavy-based saucepan over a high heat and bring to the boil. Reduce the heat to the lowest setting and simmer, stirring occasionally to break up the tamarind pulp, for 25 minutes, or until tender.

2 Tip the tamarind pulp into a sieve and use a wooden spoon to push the pulp into a clean pan.

3 Stir in the chilli, sugar and salt and continue simmering for a further 10 minutes, or until the desired consistency is reached. Leave to cool slightly, then taste and stir in extra sugar or salt if needed.

4 Leave to cool completely, then serve immediately or chill until required.

Aam ki chutney

MANGO CHUTNEY

This fresh-tasting, spiced chutney is about as far as one can get from the thick, gloopy and overly sweet mango chutney that can be bought ready-made in jars. With its punchy flavours and zingy colour, it will bring a touch of Goan sunshine to any Indian meal.

SERVES: 4–6

1 large mango, about 400 g/14 oz, peeled, stoned and finely chopped

2 tbsp lime juice

1 tbsp vegetable or groundnut oil

2 shallots, finely chopped

1 garlic clove, finely chopped

2 fresh green chillies, deseeded and finely sliced

1 tsp black mustard seeds

1 tsp coriander seeds

5 tbsp palm sugar or soft light brown sugar

5 tbsp white wine vinegar

1 tsp salt

pinch of ground ginger

PREP: 10 minutes, plus chilling time

1 Put the mango in a non-metallic bowl with the lime juice and set aside.

2 Heat the oil in a large frying pan or saucepan over a medium–high heat. Add the shallots and cook for 3 minutes. Add the garlic and chillies and stir for a further 2 minutes, or until the shallots are soft but not brown. Add the mustard seeds and coriander seeds and then stir around.

COOK: 20 minutes

3 Add the mango to the pan with the palm sugar, vinegar, salt and ground ginger and stir around. Reduce the heat to its lowest setting and simmer for 10 minutes, until the liquid thickens and the mango becomes sticky.

4 Remove from the heat and leave to cool completely. Transfer to an airtight container, cover and chill for around 3 days before using.

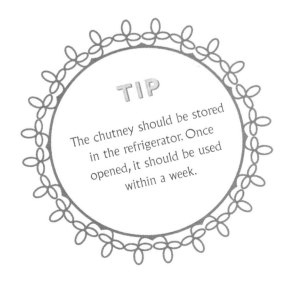

TIP

The chutney should be stored in the refrigerator. Once opened, it should be used within a week.

Nariyal sambal

COCONUT SAMBAL

Coconuts grow in abundance along the gently flowing backwaters of Kerala, and slightly crunchy fresh chutneys like this are popular. Serve as a snack with poppadoms or as an accompaniment to simply cooked seafood.

SERVES: 2–4   **PREP:** 5–10 minutes   **COOK:** 0 minutes

½ fresh coconut or 125 g / 4½ oz desiccated coconut

2 fresh green chillies, chopped (deseeded if you like)

2.5-cm / 1-inch piece fresh ginger, finely chopped

4 tbsp chopped fresh coriander

2 tbsp lemon juice, or to taste

2 shallots, very finely chopped

1 If you are using a whole coconut, use a hammer and nail to punch a hole in the 'eye' of the coconut, then pour out the water from the inside and reserve. Use the hammer to break the coconut in half, then peel and chop one half.

2 Put the chopped coconut and the chillies in a food processor and process for about 30 seconds, until finely chopped. Add the ginger, coriander and lemon juice and process again.

3 If the mixture seems too dry, stir in about 1 tablespoon of coconut water or water. Stir in the shallots and serve immediately, or cover and chill until required.

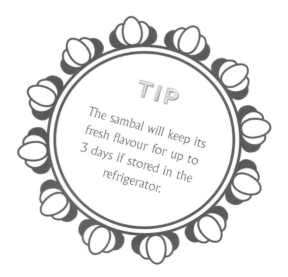

TIP

The sambal will keep its fresh flavour for up to 3 days if stored in the refrigerator.

Cuchumber

TOMATO KACHUMBAR

This popular tomato and cucumber salad is very easy to make and its vibrant colours are pleasing to the eye. It makes a refreshing accompaniment to a variety of dishes, such as grilled skewered meats.

SERVES: 6

125 ml / 4 fl oz lime juice

½ tsp sugar

pinch of salt

6 tomatoes, chopped

½ cucumber, chopped

8 spring onions, chopped

1 fresh green chilli, deseeded and chopped

1 tbsp chopped fresh coriander

1 tbsp chopped fresh mint

PREP: 10–15 minutes, plus chilling time

1 Mix together the lime juice, sugar and salt in a large bowl and stir until the sugar has completely dissolved.

2 Add the tomatoes, cucumber, spring onions, chilli, coriander and mint and toss well to mix.

COOK: 0 minutes

3 Cover and chill in the refrigerator for at least 30 minutes. Toss the salad before serving.

TIP

This salad is best eaten on the day of making, before it goes soggy. If you wish, lemon juice can be used instead of lime juice.

Nimbu ka aachar

LIME PICKLE

With chunky pieces of lime and mouth-watering spices, this tangy pickle is an ideal accompaniment to a variety of dishes. It's easy to make but requires time and patience — you'll need to start preparing it a month in advance if you plan to serve it on a particular occasion.

SERVES: 4–6

12 limes, halved and deseeded
115 g / 4 oz salt
70 g / 2½ oz chilli powder
25 g / 1 oz mustard powder
25 g / 1 oz ground fenugreek
1 tbsp ground turmeric
300 ml / 10 fl oz mustard oil
15 g / ½ oz yellow mustard seeds, crushed
½ tsp asafoetida

PREP: 10 minutes, plus marinating time

1. Cut each lime half into wedges and pack them into a large sterilized jar, sprinkling over the salt at the same time. Cover and leave to stand in a warm place for 10–14 days, or until the limes have turned brown and softened.

2. Mix together the chilli powder, mustard powder, fenugreek and turmeric in a small bowl and add to the jar of limes. Stir to mix, then re-cover and leave to stand for 2 days.

COOK: 5 minutes

3. Transfer the lime mixture to a heatproof bowl. Heat the mustard oil in a heavy-based frying pan. Add the mustard seeds and asafoetida to the pan and cook, stirring constantly, until the oil is very hot and just beginning to smoke.

4. Pour the oil and spices over the limes and mix well. Cover and leave to cool. When cool, pack into a sterilized jar, seal and store in a warm place (preferably on a sunny kitchen windowsill) for 1 week before serving.

Hari mirchi aachar

GREEN CHILLI PICKLE

This chilli pickle is a great way to spice up any meal. Indian meals are generally served with different condiments of which pickles are the most common. This is a classic hot and spicy pickle — not for the faint-hearted by any means.

SERVES: 4–6

20 fresh green chillies
3 tbsp ground coriander
1–1½ tbsp fennel seeds
1 tsp fenugreek seeds
1 tsp black mustard seeds
pinch of asafoetida
3 tsp salt
1 tsp dried mango powder (amchoor)
½ tsp ground turmeric
4 tbsp mustard oil
2 tbsp white wine vinegar

PREP: 30 minutes

1 Wash and dry the chillies and cut a slit lengthways in each.

2 Place the ground coriander, fennel seeds, fenugreek seeds and mustard seeds in a spice grinder and grind coarsely. Transfer to a bowl.

3 Add the asafoetida, salt, dried mango powder and turmeric to the bowl and mix well.

COOK: 2–3 minutes

4 Heat the oil in a frying pan until hot, then stir in the spice mixture. Cook, stirring constantly, for 1 minute and remove from the heat. Add the vinegar and stir to mix well.

5 Stuff the chillies with the spice mix and pack into a large sterilized jar. Seal and store in a warm place (preferably on a sunny kitchen windowsill) for up to 2 days before using. This pickle can be refrigerated for up to a month.

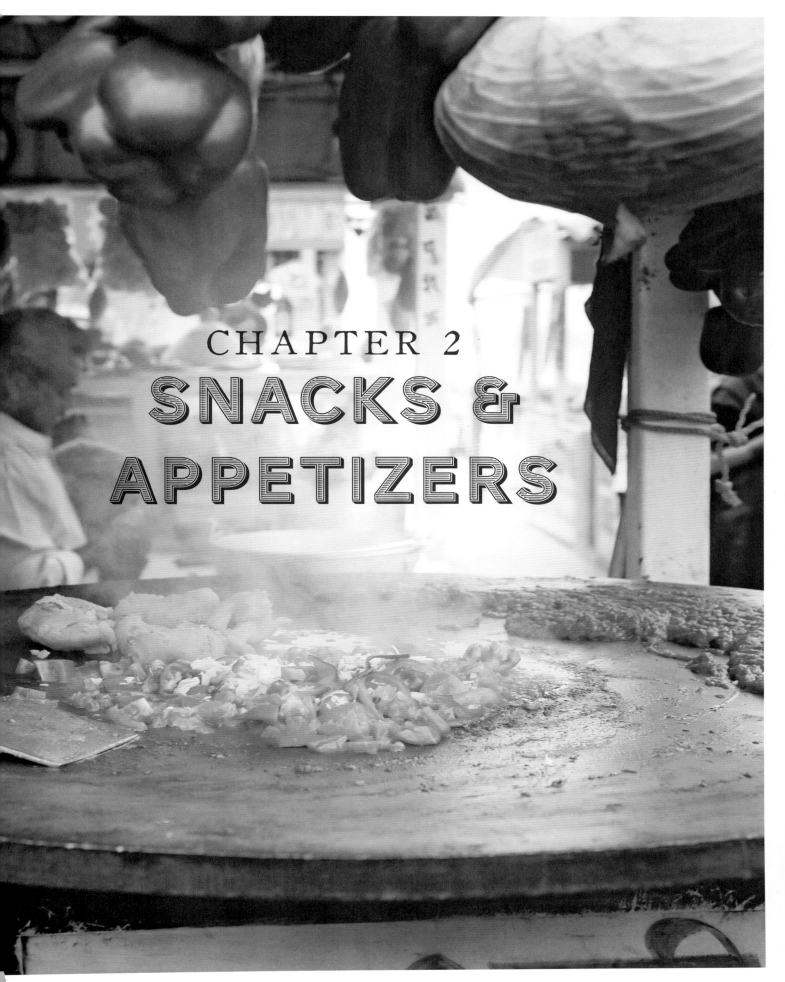

CHAPTER 2
SNACKS & APPETIZERS

Aloo mattar samosa

VEGETARIAN SAMOSAS

It takes a little practice and patience to master the art of shaping these triangular-shaped pastries, but after you've rolled out and filled a couple you will quickly get the hang of it. For a meat-based filling, try using *keema mattar* (see page 140), making sure to simmer the mixture until it is quite dry before using.

MAKES: 14

PREP: 40–45 minutes, plus resting time

COOK: 1 hour

250 g/9 oz plain flour

½ tsp salt

40 g/1½ oz ghee or butter, melted, plus extra for greasing

½ tbsp lemon juice

100–125 ml/3½–4 fl oz cold water

vegetable or groundnut oil, for deep-frying

FILLING

55 g/2 oz ghee or 4 tbsp vegetable or groundnut oil

1 onion, very finely chopped

2 garlic cloves, crushed

1 potato, very finely diced

2 carrots, very finely chopped

2 tsp mild, medium or hot curry powder, to taste

1½ tsp ground coriander

1 tsp ground turmeric

1 fresh green chilli, deseeded and finely chopped

1 tsp salt

½ tsp black mustard seeds

300 ml/10 fl oz cold water

100 g/3½ oz frozen peas

55 g/2 oz cauliflower florets, finely chopped

1 To make the filling, melt the ghee in a large frying pan over a medium–high heat. Add the onion and garlic and fry for 5–8 minutes, until soft but not brown. Stir in the potato and carrots and continue frying, stirring occasionally, for 5 minutes. Stir in the curry powder, ground coriander, turmeric, chilli, salt and mustard seeds. Pour in the water and bring to the boil. Reduce the heat to very low and simmer, uncovered, for about 15 minutes, stirring occasionally. Add the peas and cauliflower and continue simmering until all the vegetables are tender and the liquid has evaporated. Remove from the heat and set aside.

2 Meanwhile, sift the flour and salt into a bowl. Make a well in the centre, add the ghee and lemon juice and work them into the flour with your fingertips. Gradually add the water until the mixture comes together to form a soft dough. Tip the dough onto a work surface and knead for about 10 minutes, until smooth. Shape into a ball, cover with a damp tea towel and leave to rest for about 15 minutes.

3 Divide the dough into seven equal-sized pieces. Work with one piece at a time and keep the remaining pieces covered with a tea towel. On a lightly greased work surface, roll each piece of dough into a 20-cm/8-inch round, then cut in half to make two semi-circles.

4 Working with one semi-circle at a time, wet the edges with water. Place about 2 teaspoons of the filling on the dough, just off-centre. Fold one side into the centre, covering the filling. Fold the other side in the opposite direction, overlapping the first fold to form a cone shape. Wet the open edge with more water and press down to seal.

5 Heat enough oil for deep-frying in a large saucepan or deep-fryer until it reaches 180–190°C/350–375°F, or until a cube of bread browns in 30 seconds. Working in batches, deep-fry the samosas, for 2–3 minutes, flipping them over once, until golden brown. Remove with a slotted spoon and drain well on kitchen paper. Serve warm or at room temperature.

Kele ke chips

PLANTAIN CHIPS

These plantain chips are very moreish, so cook plenty. They are delicious served straight from the pan. In Kerala, unripe green bananas are cooked in the same way in coconut oil and sprinkled with salt before serving.

SERVES: 4

4 ripe plantains

1 tsp mild, medium or hot curry powder, to taste

vegetable or groundnut oil, for deep-frying

chutney, to serve

PREP: 10 minutes

1 Peel the plantains, then cut crossways into 3-mm/⅛-inch slices. Put the slices in a bowl, sprinkle over the curry powder and use your hands to toss lightly.

2 Heat enough oil for deep-frying in a large saucepan or deep-fryer to 180–190°C/350–375°F, or until a cube of bread browns in 30 seconds. Deep-fry the plantain slices, in batches, for 2 minutes, or until golden.

COOK: 10–12 minutes

3 Remove the plantain chips from the pan with a slotted spoon and drain well on kitchen paper. Serve hot with chutney.

TIP

Ordinary yellow-skinned bananas can also be used in this recipe but the flavour will be sweeter and they will take a little less time to cook.

Batata vadas
DEEP-FRIED POTATO BALLS

These savoury potato balls are eaten all over India as a snack or part of a main meal. Diced, boiled potatoes are combined with various flavourings, then rolled into balls, battered and deep-fried.

SERVES: 4

PREP: 15–20 minutes

COOK: 15–20 minutes

450 g/1 lb potatoes, boiled and diced

1 onion, chopped

2.5-cm/1-inch piece fresh ginger, finely chopped

1 fresh green chilli, deseeded and finely chopped

1 tbsp chopped fresh coriander

1 tbsp lemon juice

2 tsp dried mango powder (amchoor)

vegetable or groundnut oil, for deep-frying

salt

chutney, to serve

BATTER

115 g/4 oz gram flour

¼ tsp baking powder

¼ tsp chilli powder

pinch of salt

about 150 ml/5 fl oz cold water

1 To make the batter, sift the flour, baking powder, chilli powder and salt into a bowl. Gradually stir in enough of the water to make a smooth batter. Cover with clingfilm and set aside.

2 Place the potatoes, onion, ginger, chilli, coriander, lemon juice and dried mango powder in a separate bowl. Mix well with a wooden spoon, breaking up the potatoes. Season with salt to taste. Break off small pieces of the mixture and form into balls between the palms of your hands.

3 Heat enough oil for deep-frying in a large saucepan or deep-fryer to 180–190°C/350–375°F, or until a cube of bread browns in 30 seconds. Working in batches, dip the potato balls in the batter, using a fork, and add to the hot oil. Deep-fry for 3–4 minutes, until golden brown. Remove with a slotted spoon and drain on kitchen paper. Serve hot with chutney.

TIP
It is best to allow the boiled potatoes to cool before combining them with the other ingredients because this will result in firmer potato balls.

Mirchi pakora

STUFFED CHILLI BHAJIS

Also called *mirapakaya bajjilu* or *bajji* in Telagu, this snack of chillies stuffed with a spiced potato mixture is a speciality from Andhra Pradesh in central India and is classic street food. Serve it with your favourite chutney or a little natural yogurt.

MAKES: 8

PREP: 20 minutes, plus soaking time

COOK: 10 minutes

8 large, mild fresh green chillies

vegetable or groundnut oil, for deep-frying

BATTER

250 g/9 oz gram flour

125 g/4½ oz rice flour

½ tsp baking powder

1 tsp ground cumin

2 tsp salt

1 tsp chilli powder

about 700 ml/1¼ pints cold water

STUFFING

2 tbsp vegetable or groundnut oil

1 tsp fennel seeds

2 tsp black mustard seeds

1 tsp cumin seeds

1 potato, peeled, boiled and mashed

3 tbsp finely chopped fresh coriander

1 tsp salt

½ tsp tamarind paste

1 tbsp roasted peanuts, roughly chopped

1 Slit the chillies lengthways and remove all the seeds using a small teaspoon. Soak the chillies in boiling water for 5 minutes. Drain on kitchen paper and set aside.

2 Mix together the batter ingredients with enough of the water to make a thin batter with the consistency of double cream. Set aside.

3 For the stuffing, heat the oil in a pan. Add the fennel seeds, mustard seeds and cumin seeds. When the seeds start to pop, add the potato, coriander and salt and mix well. Add the tamarind paste and sprinkle over the roasted peanuts. Remove from the heat and mash until evenly combined.

4 Using your fingers, stuff the green chillies with the potato mixture.

5 Heat enough oil for deep-frying in a large saucepan or deep-fryer to 180–190°C/350–375°F, or until a cube of bread browns in 30 seconds. Working in batches, dip the stuffed green chillies in the batter and deep-fry, for 2–3 minutes, or until crisp and golden. Remove with a slotted spoon and drain on kitchen paper. Serve warm.

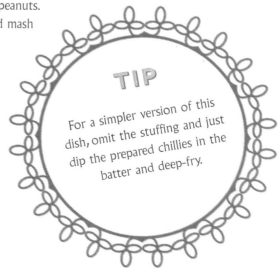

TIP

For a simpler version of this dish, omit the stuffing and just dip the prepared chillies in the batter and deep-fry.

खान म

KHAN M

←

हिट कि

MARKET

Khandvi

SPICED GRAM FLOUR ROLLS

Making these delicate and delicious lightly spiced gram flour rolls from Gujarat is almost like making an Indian-style pasta. There is an art to making and rolling the *khandvi* and it may take more than a few attempts to get the perfect-looking ones, although the taste will be great every time.

MAKES: 24

vegetable or groundnut oil, for greasing
250 g/9 oz gram flour, sifted
100 g/3½ oz set natural yogurt
600 ml/1 pint warm water
2 tsp salt
¼ tsp ground turmeric
2 tsp grated fresh ginger
2 garlic cloves, crushed
4 tsp green chilli paste (see page 26)

TOPPING

6 tbsp vegetable or groundnut oil
1 tsp sesame seeds
1 tsp black mustard seeds
4 tbsp finely chopped fresh coriander
2 tbsp freshly grated coconut

PREP: 15–20 minutes

1 Lightly brush four large baking trays with oil and set aside.

2 Place the gram flour, yogurt and water in a heavy-based saucepan with the salt, turmeric, ginger, garlic and green chilli paste. Whisk until smooth, then place over a medium heat and continue to whisk constantly. When the batter starts to thicken (after about 5–6 minutes), reduce the heat to low, cover and cook for 4–5 minutes. Stir, re-cover and cook for a further 2–3 minutes, or until thickened and smooth.

3 Remove from the heat and ladle the batter onto the prepared baking trays, using a palette knife to spread the mixture as thinly as possible. The batter will start to set as it cools. Leave to stand for 5 minutes, then slice it lengthways into 5 cm/2 inch wide strips. This quantity should make about 24 rolls.

COOK: 20 minutes, plus standing time

4 Starting at one end of each strip, use the palette knife to gently lift and roll (like a small Swiss roll). Repeat until all the strips have been rolled. Transfer to a serving plate.

5 Meanwhile, make the topping. Heat the oil in a frying pan and add the sesame seeds and mustard seeds. When they start to pop, remove from the heat and drizzle this spiced oil over the gram flour rolls. Sprinkle over the coriander and coconut. Serve warm or at room temperature.

Sabudana aloo wada

TAPIOCA & POTATO CAKES

These savoury potato and tapioca cakes from western and southern India are usually served as a snack with *masala chai* (tea). Tapioca pearls are made from a starch extracted from the cassava root. They come in various sizes and can be found in any Asian grocery store.

MAKES: 15–20

PREP: 10–15 minutes, plus soaking time

COOK: 25–30 minutes

2 potatoes, peeled and roughly chopped
200 g/7 oz medium-sized tapioca pearls
250 ml/9 fl oz cold water
2 fresh red chillies, finely chopped
1 tsp cumin seeds
1 tsp salt
4 tbsp finely chopped fresh coriander
vegetable or groundnut oil, for deep-frying

1 Place the potatoes in a pan of boiling water. Boil for 12–15 minutes, or until just tender. Drain thoroughly and transfer to a mixing bowl.

2 Meanwhile, place the tapioca in a bowl and pour over the water. Leave to soak for 12–15 minutes, or until the water has been absorbed and the tapioca is swollen. Transfer to a sieve to drain away any excess liquid.

3 Add the chillies, cumin seeds, salt and coriander to the potatoes and mash until fairly smooth. Stir in the soaked tapioca and stir to mix well. With wet hands, roll the mixture into 15–20 walnut-sized balls, then flatten to make patties.

4 Heat enough oil for deep-frying in a large saucepan or deep-fryer to 180–190°C/350–375°F, or until a cube of bread browns in 30 seconds. Working in batches, deep-fry the tapioca and potato cakes, for 3–4 minutes, or until golden brown. Remove with a slotted spoon and drain on kitchen paper. Serve warm.

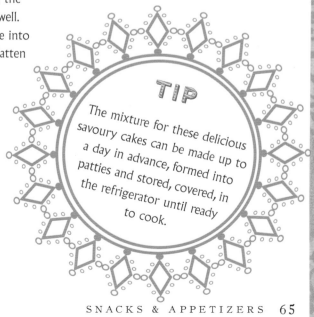

TIP

The mixture for these delicious savoury cakes can be made up to a day in advance, formed into patties and stored, covered, in the refrigerator until ready to cook.

Paneer tikka
PANEER TIKKA

For India's millions of vegetarians, *paneer* (a firm, white cheese) is the main source of dietary protein. It has very little taste on its own, which is why it is paired here with a hot, spicy tikka paste.

MAKES: 4

PREP: 15–20 minutes, plus marinating time

COOK: 15–20 minutes

350 g/12 oz paneer, cut into 16 cubes
vegetable or groundnut oil, for brushing
1 tsp garam masala
fresh coriander leaves, to garnish

TIKKA PASTE

10 black peppercorns
6 cloves
seeds from 4 green cardamom pods
1 tsp cumin seeds
1 tsp coriander seeds
½ tsp poppy seeds
½ tsp chilli powder
½ tsp ground turmeric
1 tbsp garlic paste
1 tbsp ginger paste
½ small onion, chopped
150 g/5½ oz wholemilk natural yogurt
½ tbsp tomato purée
1 tbsp gram flour
1 tbsp vegetable or groundnut oil

1 To make the tikka paste, dry-fry the peppercorns, cloves, cardamom seeds, cumin seeds, coriander seeds and poppy seeds in a frying pan over a high heat, stirring constantly, until you can smell the aroma. Immediately tip out of the pan so they don't burn.

2 Put the spices in a spice grinder or use a pestle and mortar. Add the chilli powder and turmeric and grind to a fine powder. Add the garlic paste, ginger paste and onion and continue grinding until a paste forms. Transfer to a large bowl and stir in the yogurt, tomato purée, gram flour and oil.

3 Add the paneer to the bowl and use your hands to coat the cubes in the tikka paste, taking care not to break up the pieces of cheese. Leave to marinate at room temperature for 30 minutes, or cover the bowl with clingfilm and chill for up to 24 hours.

4 Preheat the grill to medium–high. If you have refrigerated the cheese remove it from the refrigerator 15 minutes before cooking. Lightly brush four metal skewers with oil. Drain the paneer and thread onto the skewers, leaving a little space between each cube.

5 Cook the skewers under the preheated grill for 12–15 minutes, turning them over once and basting with any remaining tikka paste, until the paneer is lightly charred on the edges.

6 To serve, sprinkle the hot kebabs with the garam masala and garnish with coriander leaves.

Gobhi ka pakora

GOLDEN CAULIFLOWER FRITTERS

These golden fritters are made from cauliflower florets dipped into a spiced batter and deep-fried until crisp. They are delicious as a snack, served with chutney for dipping, or as part of a meal.

SERVES: 4

PREP: 10–15 minutes, plus standing time

COOK: 20–25 minutes

vegetable or groundnut oil, for deep-frying

400 g/14 oz cauliflower florets

chutney, to serve

BATTER

140 g/5 oz gram flour

2 tsp ground coriander

1 tsp garam masala

1 tsp salt

½ tsp ground turmeric

pinch of chilli powder

15 g/½ oz ghee, melted, or 1 tbsp vegetable or groundnut oil

1 tsp lemon juice

150 ml/5 fl oz cold water

2 tsp nigella seeds

1 To make the batter, stir the gram flour, ground coriander, garam masala, salt, turmeric and chilli powder into a large bowl. Make a well in the centre, add the ghee and lemon juice with 2 tablespoons of the water and stir to make a thick batter. Slowly beat in enough of the remaining water with an electric hand-held mixer or a whisk to make a smooth batter with the consistency of double cream. Stir in the nigella seeds. Cover the bowl with clingfilm and set aside for at least 30 minutes.

2 Heat enough oil for deep-frying in a large saucepan or deep-fryer to 180–190°C/350–375°F, or until a cube of bread browns in 30 seconds. Dip one cauliflower floret at a time into the batter and allow any excess batter to drip back into the bowl, then drop the cauliflower floret into the hot oil. Add a few more batter-dipped cauliflower florets, without overcrowding the pan, and fry for about 3 minutes, or until golden brown and crisp.

3 Use a slotted spoon to remove the fritters from the oil and drain well on kitchen paper. Continue frying until all the cauliflower florets and batter have been used. Serve the fritters with chutney for dipping.

Pyaaz pakora

SPICY ONION FRITTERS

These seriously tasty spiced onion fritters are extremely difficult to resist! They are a popular snack all over India and can often be found among the foods on offer from the roadside stalls or carts of the numerous street vendors. They are best enjoyed with chutney for dipping.

SERVES: 4

PREP: 10–15 minutes

COOK: 25–30 minutes

150 g/5½ oz gram flour

1 tsp salt, or to taste

small pinch of bicarbonate of soda

25 g/1 oz ground rice

1 tsp fennel seeds

1 tsp cumin seeds

2 fresh green chillies, finely chopped (deseeded if you like)

2 large onions (about 400 g/14 oz), sliced into half-rings and separated

15 g/½ oz fresh coriander, leaves and stalks, finely chopped

200 ml/7 fl oz cold water

vegetable or groundnut oil, for deep-frying

1 Sift the gram flour into a large bowl and add the salt, bicarbonate of soda, ground rice, fennel seeds and cumin seeds. Mix together well, then add the chillies, onions and coriander. Gradually pour in the water and mix until a thick batter is formed and the onions are thoroughly coated with it.

2 Heat enough oil for deep-frying in a large saucepan or deep-fryer to 180–190°C/350–375°F, or until a cube of bread browns in 30 seconds. Add as many small amounts (each about ½ tablespoon) of the batter as will fit in a single layer, without overcrowding the pan. Reduce the heat slightly and cook the fritters for 8–10 minutes, until golden brown and crisp.

3 Use a slotted spoon to remove the fritters from the oil and drain well on kitchen paper. Continue frying until all the batter mixture has been used. Serve hot.

Kadhi
SPICED YOGURT SOUP

Kadhi is a traditional Gujarati preparation of a wonderful sweet and spicy yogurt mixture thickened with gram flour. This authentic Gujarati-style spiced yogurt soup is slightly thinner in texture than the Punjabi version of the same dish. They both have a balance of sweet, sour and spicy flavours.

SERVES: 4　　　**PREP:** 20 minutes　　　**COOK:** 15–20 minutes

1 litre/1¾ pints cold water

500 g/1 lb 2 oz wholemilk natural yogurt

3 tbsp gram flour

4 fresh green chillies, slit lengthways

1 tbsp freshly grated ginger

1 tbsp palm sugar

1 tsp ground turmeric

1 tbsp vegetable or groundnut oil

1 tbsp ghee

2 dried red chillies, broken into pieces

8 fresh curry leaves

1 tsp cumin seeds

½ tsp black mustard seeds

pinch of asafoetida

4 tbsp chopped fresh coriander

salt

1 Mix together the water, yogurt and gram flour in a large saucepan until smooth. Add the green chillies, ginger, palm sugar, turmeric and salt to taste. Bring the mixture to the boil, then immediately reduce the heat to low and cook, stirring frequently, for about 8–10 minutes.

2 Meanwhile, heat the oil and ghee in a small frying pan over a medium heat. Add the dried red chillies, curry leaves, cumin seeds, mustard seeds and asafoetida and cook, stirring constantly, for 2–3 minutes, or until the seeds start to pop.

3 Stir the spiced oil into the yogurt mixture in the saucepan. Ladle into warmed bowls, scatter over the coriander and serve hot.

TIP

For a thicker version of this soup, increase the quantity of gram flour to 5 tablespoons. Be careful not to boil the yogurt for too long or it will curdle.

Pao bhaji

SPICED POTATO & VEGETABLE SNACK

This incredibly popular street snack originated in Mumbai, but is now prevalent throughout India. It consists of a mixed potato and vegetable mixture and is served with warmed buns or *pao*. *Pao bhaji masala* is a ready-made spice mixture that is readily available in Asian grocery stores.

SERVES: 4

PREP: 25 minutes

COOK: 45–50 minutes

4 tbsp vegetable or groundnut oil

50 g/1¾ oz butter

2 garlic cloves, crushed

2 fresh green chillies, finely chopped

1 large onion, finely chopped

2 tsp grated fresh ginger

400 g/14 oz canned chopped tomatoes

200 g/7 oz cauliflower, finely chopped

100 g/3½ oz green cabbage, finely chopped

200 g/7 oz fresh shelled or frozen peas

1 large carrot, coarsely grated

4 potatoes, boiled, peeled and mashed

3 tbsp pao bhaji masala (see page 28)

2 tsp salt

1 tbsp lemon juice

4 tbsp finely chopped fresh coriander

4 white rolls, to serve

1 Heat the oil and butter in a wok or large frying pan over a medium heat. Sauté the garlic and chillies for 30 seconds, then stir in the onion and ginger. Stir-fry for 8–10 minutes, or until the onion is lightly browned.

2 Add the tomatoes and stir-fry for 6–8 minutes, or until thickened. Stir in the cauliflower, cabbage, peas, carrot and potatoes. Add the pao bhaji masala. Cover and cook, stirring occasionally, for 15–20 minutes.

3 Preheat the grill. Season the potato and vegetable mixture with the salt and stir in the lemon juice. Remove from the heat and scatter over the chopped coriander. Split the rolls in half and lightly toast them under the preheated grill. Serve the potato mixture in warmed bowls with the toasted rolls.

Macchi pakora

GOLDEN FISH FRITTERS

These fish fritters make the most of the abundance of fresh fish in India's coastal regions. They are coated in a lightly spiced gram flour batter and deep-fried until crisp and golden.

SERVES: 4–6

PREP: 10–15 minutes, plus marinating time

COOK: 15–20 minutes

½ tsp salt

2 tbsp lemon juice or white wine vinegar

700 g/1 lb 9 oz skinless white fish fillets, such as cod, halibut or monkfish, cut into large chunks

vegetable or groundnut oil, for deep-frying

pepper

lemon wedges, to serve

BATTER

140 g/5 oz gram flour

seeds from 4 green cardamom pods

large pinch of ground turmeric

large pinch of bicarbonate of soda

finely grated rind of 1 lemon

175 ml/6 fl oz cold water

salt and pepper

1 Combine the salt and lemon juice in a small bowl with pepper to taste. Rub this mixture all over the fish chunks, then transfer to a non-metallic bowl and leave to marinate for 20–30 minutes.

2 Meanwhile, to make the batter put the gram flour in a bowl and stir in the cardamom seeds, turmeric, bicarbonate of soda, lemon rind and salt and pepper to taste. Make a well in the centre and gradually stir in the water to make a thin batter with the consistency of single cream.

3 Gently stir the pieces of fish into the batter, taking care not to break them up.

4 Heat enough oil for deep-frying in a large saucepan or deep-fryer to 180–190°C/350–375°F, or until a cube of bread browns in 30 seconds. Remove the fish pieces from the batter and allow the excess batter to drip back into the bowl. Working in batches, drop the battered fish pieces into the hot oil and deep-fry for about 2½–3 minutes, until golden brown.

5 Use a slotted spoon to remove the fried fish pieces from the oil and drain on kitchen paper. Continue frying until all the fish has been used. Serve hot with lemon wedges for squeezing over.

Mahi tikka
FISH TIKKA

You need a firm-fleshed fish for these delectable fish skewers — salmon has been used here, but monkfish would work equally well. Traditionally, these would be cooked in a *tandoor* (Indian clay oven).

MAKES: 8

PREP: 10–15 minutes, plus soaking & marinating time

COOK: 10 minutes, plus standing time

pinch of saffron threads, pounded

1 tbsp hot milk

85 g/3 oz Greek-style yogurt

1 tbsp garlic paste

1 tbsp ginger paste

1 tsp salt, or to taste

½ tsp sugar

juice of ½ lemon

½–1 tsp chilli powder

½ tsp garam masala

1 tsp ground fennel seeds

2 tsp gram flour

750 g/1 lb 10 oz salmon fillets, skinned and cut into 5-cm/2-inch cubes

3 tbsp vegetable or groundnut oil, plus extra for brushing

1 Soak the pounded saffron in the hot milk for 10 minutes.

2 Put all the remaining ingredients, except the fish and oil, in a bowl and beat with a fork or a whisk until smooth. Add the saffron and milk mixture, stir well and add the fish cubes. Using a metal spoon, mix gently, turning the fish around until fully coated with the marinade. Cover and leave to marinate in the refrigerator for 2 hours. Return to room temperature before cooking.

3 Preheat the grill to high. Brush the grill rack generously with oil. Brush eight metal skewers lightly with oil.

4 Thread the fish cubes onto the prepared skewers, leaving a little space between each piece. Arrange on the prepared grill rack and cook under the preheated grill for 3 minutes. Brush half the oil over the kebabs and cook for a further minute. Turn over and brush any remaining marinade over the fish. Cook for 3 minutes. Brush the remaining oil over the fish and cook for a further 2 minutes, or until the fish is lightly charred.

5 Remove the skewers from the heat and leave to stand for 5 minutes before serving.

Jhinga poori

PRAWN POORIS

In this recipe, deep-fried wholemeal flatbreads, or pooris, are topped with a spicy prawn and tomato mixture. Pooris are best served straight from the pan so, if you want to avoid last-minute deep-frying, you could use chapattis or naans instead.

MAKES: 6

PREP: 10 minutes

COOK: 15–20 minutes

2 tsp coriander seeds

½ tsp black peppercorns

1 large garlic clove, crushed

1 tsp ground turmeric

¼–½ tsp chilli powder

½ tsp salt, or to taste

40 g/1½ oz ghee or 3 tbsp vegetable or groundnut oil

1 onion, grated

800 g/1 lb 12 oz canned crushed tomatoes

pinch of sugar

500 g/1 lb 2 oz small cooked peeled prawns, thawed if frozen

½ tsp garam masala, plus extra to garnish

6 pooris, kept warm (see page 191)

fresh chopped coriander, to garnish

1 Put the coriander seeds, peppercorns, garlic, turmeric, chilli powder and salt in a small food processor or spice grinder and blend to a thick paste. Alternatively, use a mortar and pestle.

2 Melt the ghee in a wok or large frying pan over a low–medium heat. Add the spice paste and cook, stirring constantly, for about 30 seconds.

3 Add the grated onion and stir around for a further 30 seconds. Stir in the tomatoes and the sugar. Bring to the boil, stirring and mashing the tomatoes against the side of the pan to break them down, and simmer for 10 minutes, or until reduced. Taste and adjust the seasoning, adding extra salt if needed.

4 Add the prawns and sprinkle with the garam masala. When the prawns are hot, arrange the warm pooris on plates and top each with a portion of prawns. Sprinkle with the chopped coriander and garam masala and serve immediately.

Jhinga masala vadas

MASALA PRAWN CAKES

Perfect as canapés, these Goan-inspired prawn cakes are packed with the punchy, fresh flavours of garlic, ginger, coconut, chilli, coriander and mint. Squeeze over a little fresh lime juice to add even more zing and serve with a refreshing chilled drink.

MAKES: 20

PREP: 20 minutes, plus chilling time

COOK: 12–15 minutes

4 tbsp vegetable or groundnut oil
lime wedges, to serve

PRAWN CAKES

800 g/1 lb 12 oz raw tiger prawns, peeled and deveined

2 fresh red chillies, deseeded and very finely chopped

6 tbsp finely chopped fresh coriander

6 tbsp finely chopped fresh mint

1 tsp coconut cream

4 spring onions, finely sliced

2 garlic cloves, finely chopped

2 tsp finely grated fresh ginger

8 tbsp fresh white breadcrumbs

2 tsp ground cumin

1 tsp chilli powder

1 small egg, lightly beaten

1 To make the prawn cakes, roughly chop the prawns and place them in a food processor with the remaining ingredients. Blend to a coarse paste. Transfer the mixture to a bowl, cover and chill in the refrigerator for at least 6–8 hours, or overnight.

2 Preheat the oven to 200°C/400°F/ Gas Mark 6. Line a baking tray with baking paper.

3 Shape the fish mixture into 20 small patties, approximately 4 cm/1½ inches in diameter. Place on the prepared baking tray and lightly brush with the oil. Bake in the preheated oven for 12–15 minutes, or until slightly puffed up and light golden.

4 Serve warm or at room temperature with lime wedges for squeezing over.

TIP
To make masala fish cakes, simply replace the prawns with roughly chopped white fish fillet (such as cod or haddock).

Samudrapheni masala

CRISPY CHILLI SQUID

This quick and easy starter is inspired by the cuisine of the Konkan Coast, a rugged stretch of the coastline of western India rich in natural beauty. Serve these delectable morsels on their own or with steamed rice and a mild lentil curry or dal.

SERVES: 4

PREP: 20 minutes, plus marinating time

COOK: 10–12 minutes

500 g/1 lb 2 oz prepared squid rings
5 tbsp semolina
6 tbsp cornflour
vegetable or groundnut oil, for deep-frying

MARINADE

3 fresh red chillies, finely chopped
2 tsp finely grated fresh ginger
3 garlic cloves, crushed
2 tbsp white wine vinegar
4 tbsp vegetable or groundnut oil
1 tsp ground cumin
1 tsp crushed coriander seeds
1 tsp salt

1 Place all the marinade ingredients in a small food processor and blend until smooth. Transfer to a shallow, non-metallic dish and add the squid rings. Toss to mix well, cover and leave to marinate in the refrigerator for 1 hour.

2 In a separate bowl, mix together the semolina and cornflour. Set aside.

3 Heat enough oil for deep-frying in a large saucepan or deep-fryer to 180–190°C/350–375°F, or until a cube of bread browns in 30 seconds. Remove the squid from its marinade and toss it in the semolina mixture to coat. Shake off any excess and deep-fry the squid, in batches, for 1–2 minutes, or until crisp and golden.

4 Remove the squid with a slotted spoon and drain on kitchen paper. Serve immediately.

TIP

For crispy chilli prawns, replace the squid with raw peeled and deveined tiger prawns.

Gosht hara kabab

CORIANDER LAMB KEBABS

These fragrant and subtly spiced kebabs are traditionally cooked in a tandoor oven to produce a dry exterior whilst keeping the centre tender. Cooking them under a hot grill or over glowing coals also gives good results.

MAKES: 6

PREP: 15–20 minutes, plus standing time

COOK: 5–7 minutes

700 g/1 lb 9 oz fresh lamb mince

1 onion, grated

3 tbsp finely chopped fresh coriander, leaves and stems

3 tbsp finely chopped fresh mint

3 tbsp gram flour

1½ tbsp ground almonds

2.5-cm/1-inch piece fresh ginger, grated

3 tbsp lemon juice

2 tbsp wholemilk natural yogurt

2 tsp ground cumin

2 tsp ground coriander

1½ tsp salt

1½ tsp garam masala

1 tsp ground cinnamon

½ tsp pepper

vegetable or groundnut oil, for brushing

1 Place all the ingredients, except the oil, in a large bowl and use your hands to mix together until combined and smooth. Cover the bowl with clingfilm and leave to stand at room temperature for about 45 minutes.

2 With wet hands, divide the lamb mixture into 24 equal-sized balls. Thread four balls onto each of six metal skewers, leaving a little space between each one.

3 Preheat the grill to high or light barbecue coals and leave to burn until they turn grey. Lightly brush the grill rack or barbecue rack with oil. Add the skewers and grill, turning frequently, for 5–7 minutes, until the lamb is completely cooked through and not at all pink when you pierce it with the point of a knife. Serve immediately.

Boti shashlik

MARINATED LAMB BROCHETTES

In this recipe, tender cubes of lamb are infused with a spiced yogurt marinade, skewered with red peppers and shallots, and grilled. Make sure to trim off any excess fat from the meat before cutting it into cubes.

MAKES: 4

700 g/1 lb 9 oz boned leg of lamb, cut into 2.5-cm/1-inch cubes

2 tbsp light malt vinegar

½ tsp salt, or to taste

1 tbsp garlic paste

1 tbsp ginger paste

115 g/4 oz wholemilk natural yogurt, strained, or Greek-style yogurt

1 tbsp gram flour

1 tsp ground cumin

1 tsp garam masala

½–1 tsp chilli powder

½ tsp ground turmeric

3 tbsp vegetable or groundnut oil, plus extra for brushing

½ red pepper, deseeded and cut into 2.5-cm/1-inch pieces

½ green pepper, deseeded and cut into 2.5-cm/1-inch pieces

8 shallots, halved

55 g/2 oz butter, melted

PREP: 15–20 minutes, plus marinating time

1 Put the meat in a large, non-metallic bowl and add the vinegar, salt, garlic paste and ginger paste. Mix together thoroughly, cover and leave to marinate in the refrigerator for 30 minutes.

2 Put the yogurt and gram flour in a separate bowl and beat together with a fork until smooth. Add the cumin, garam masala, chilli powder, turmeric and oil and mix together thoroughly. Add the yogurt mixture to the marinated meat, then add the peppers and shallots and stir until well blended. Cover and leave to marinate in the refrigerator for 2–3 hours, or overnight. Return to room temperature before cooking.

3 Preheat the grill to high. Brush the grill rack and four metal skewers with oil.

COOK: 11–12 minutes, plus standing time

4 Thread the marinated lamb, peppers and shallots alternately onto the prepared skewers. Place the skewers on the prepared grill rack and cook under the preheated grill for 4 minutes. Brush generously with half the melted butter and cook for a further 2 minutes. Turn over and cook for 3–4 minutes. Brush with the remaining butter and cook for a further 2 minutes.

5 Balance the brochettes over a large saucepan or frying pan and leave to stand for 5–6 minutes before sliding off the skewers with a knife. Serve immediately.

Kathi roll

CHICKEN & EGG ROLLS

In Bengal, these egg-based pancakes are served as street-side snacks. They can be filled with spiced vegetables, paneer or meat — here they are stuffed with marinated, grilled chicken. For extra zing, add a couple of tablespoons of coriander chutney (see page 40) to the filling.

MAKES: 6

PREP: 30 minutes, plus marinating time

COOK: 25–30 minutes

2 skinless, boneless chicken breasts, cut into bite-sized pieces

200 g/7 oz plain flour, plus extra for dusting

1 tsp salt

1 tbsp vegetable or groundnut oil

100 ml/3½ fl oz milk

4 eggs

fresh mint leaves and sliced red onion, to serve

MARINADE

2 garlic cloves, crushed

1 tsp grated fresh ginger

2 tsp ground cumin

1 tsp chilli powder

¼ tsp ground turmeric

¼ tsp garam masala

2 tsp tomato purée

2 tbsp wholemilk natural yogurt

1 tbsp lemon juice

1 tsp salt

1 tbsp vegetable or groundnut oil

1 Place all the marinade ingredients in a non-metallic bowl with the chicken and stir to mix well. Cover and chill in the refrigerator for 6–8 hours, or overnight if possible.

2 When ready to cook, preheat the grill to medium–high. Thread the marinated chicken onto metal skewers. Place the chicken skewers on a grill rack and cook under the preheated grill, turning once, for 12–15 minutes, until cooked through and tender. Remove the chicken from the skewers and keep warm.

3 Meanwhile, sift the flour and salt into a large bowl. Add the oil, milk and one of the eggs and knead for 8–10 minutes, until smooth. Form into a ball, cover and leave to rest for 15–20 minutes.

4 Divide the dough into six equal-sized pieces and form each into a ball. On a lightly floured surface, roll each ball into a round that is 16–17 cm/6¼–6½ inches in diameter and about 3 mm/⅛ inch thick. Lightly beat the remaining eggs.

5 Heat a non-stick frying pan over a medium heat. Working one at a time, place a dough round in the pan and cook for 1 minute. Flip it over and spread 1 tablespoon of the beaten egg all over the surface. Immediately flip it over again and cook for 30–40 seconds, then remove from the heat. Repeat until all the dough rounds have been cooked.

6 Divide the chicken between the egg rolls and scatter over a few mint leaves and some sliced red onion. Roll tightly to enclose the filling and serve immediately.

Murgh momo

STEAMED CHICKEN DUMPLINGS

Very popular in Darjeeling (the hill station in West Bengal), these steamed stuffed chicken dumplings are an example of the Nepalese and Tibetan influences on Indian cuisine due to the close proximity of these two countries.

MAKES: 20

PREP: 30 minutes, plus marinating & resting time

COOK: 12–15 minutes

1 tbsp white wine vinegar

1 tbsp dark soy sauce

6 spring onions, very finely chopped

2 garlic cloves, crushed

2 tsp salt

2 fresh green chillies, finely chopped

200 g/7 oz fresh chicken mince

150 g/5½ oz plain flour, plus extra for dusting

5 tbsp tepid water

2 tbsp vegetable or groundnut oil, plus extra for brushing

sweet chilli sauce, to serve

1 Mix together the vinegar, soy sauce, spring onions, garlic, 1 teaspoon of the salt and the chillies in a bowl. Add the chicken mince and, using your fingers, mix until well combined. Cover and leave to marinate for 30 minutes.

2 Meanwhile, sift the flour and the remaining salt into a large bowl. Add the water and oil and knead for 8–10 minutes to make a soft dough. Cover and leave to rest for 15–20 minutes.

3 Divide the dough into 20 small balls. On a lightly floured surface, roll each ball out into a very thin round that is 10 cm/4 inches in diameter and about 1 mm/3⁄64 inch thick.

4 Place a little of the chicken mixture in the centre of each dough round. Fold in half to make a semi-circular dumpling, sealing it tightly by carefully pinching the folded edges together.

5 Place the dumplings in a single layer in a steamer and lightly brush with oil. Steam over a high heat for 12–15 minutes, or until the chicken is cooked through. Serve warm with sweet chilli sauce.

TIP

You can make these dumplings up to a day in advance and steam them when you are ready to serve.

CHAPTER 3
MAIN DISHES

Thukpa

VEGETABLE NOODLE BROTH

This hearty vegetarian version of a popular noodle-based broth is another example of the influence of Tibetan cuisine in the Bengal region. It is a favourite amongst students and is served in many school and college canteens.

SERVES: 4

PREP: 20–25 minutes

COOK: 25–30 minutes

400 g/14 oz dried thick egg noodles

2 tbsp vegetable or groundnut oil

1 onion, finely chopped

1 tsp ground cumin

½ tsp ground turmeric

2 garlic cloves, crushed

2 tsp grated fresh ginger

1 tsp salt

2 fresh green chillies, finely chopped

100 g/3½ oz mangetout, thinly sliced lengthways

2 large carrots, cut into matchsticks

1 red pepper, deseeded and thinly sliced

2 tomatoes, finely chopped

2 tbsp dark soy sauce

1 litre/1¾ pints vegetable stock

1 tsp pepper

200 g/7 oz baby spinach leaves

6 tbsp finely chopped fresh coriander

1 tsp toasted sesame oil

1 Cook the noodles according to the packet instructions. Drain, rinse with cold water and set aside.

2 Meanwhile, heat the vegetable oil in a large saucepan over a medium heat, add the onion and stir-fry for 8–10 minutes, or until lightly browned.

3 Add the cumin, turmeric, garlic, ginger, salt and chillies to the pan and stir-fry for 1–2 minutes. Add the mangetout, carrots and red pepper and stir-fry for a further 1–2 minutes.

4 Add the tomatoes, soy sauce, stock and pepper. Bring to the boil, then reduce the heat and simmer for 10–12 minutes, until the vegetables are tender.

5 Add the reserved noodles and the spinach and bring back to the boil. Stir until the spinach wilts, then remove from the heat and stir in the chopped coriander and sesame oil. Ladle into bowls and serve immediately.

Shukto

BENGALI VEGETABLE CURRY

A traditional Bengali vegetable curry, *shukto* uses a mixture of chopped vegetables and is cooked with a mustard seed and white poppy seed paste. *Panch phoran* is a Bengali spice mixture made up of equal quantities of fenugreek seeds, fennel seeds, mustard seeds, nigella seeds and cumin seeds.

SERVES: 4

PREP: 30 minutes, plus soaking time

COOK: 25–30 minutes

6 tbsp white poppy seeds (khus khus)

3 tbsp black mustard seeds

2 tsp grated fresh ginger

4 tbsp vegetable or groundnut oil

2 fresh green chillies, split lengthways

1 tbsp panch phoran

200 g/7 oz fresh bittergourd (kerala), cut into 1.5-cm/⅝-inch cubes

2 potatoes, peeled and cut into 1.5-cm/⅝-inch cubes

1 aubergine, cut into 1.5-cm/⅝-inch cubes

1 courgette, cut into 1.5-cm/⅝-inch cubes

1 carrot, cut into 1.5-cm/⅝-inch cubes

1 tomato, finely chopped

100 g/3½ oz fresh or frozen peas

400 ml/14 fl oz cold water

¼ tsp ground turmeric

2 tsp salt

1 tsp palm sugar

125 ml/4 fl oz milk

1 Soak the white poppy seeds and 2 tablespoons of the mustard seeds in warm water for 1 hour. Drain and blend with the ginger to make a paste.

2 Heat the oil in a large frying pan and add the remaining mustard seeds and the chillies. When the mustard seeds start to pop, add the panch phoran and all the vegetables. Add half the water and stir to mix well, then cover tightly and cook, stirring frequently, over a medium heat for 10–12 minutes.

3 Add half the white poppy seed and mustard seed paste, the turmeric and salt. Add the remaining water and cook, stirring frequently, over a low–medium heat for a further 10–15 minutes.

4 Add the remaining white poppy seed and mustard seed paste, the palm sugar and milk and cook for a further 5 minutes, or until the vegetables are tender. Serve hot.

TIP

If you cannot find bittergourd, replace with peeled and deseeded butternut squash or pumpkin.

Sambhar

SOUTH INDIAN LENTIL & VEGETABLE CURRY

This light soup-like lentil curry from Tamil Nadu is probably the most typical dish of south India. With a large vegetarian population in the region, most people will eat one version or another of this every day.

SERVES: 4–6

PREP: 15–20 minutes, plus soaking time

COOK: 30–35 minutes

250 g/9 oz split red lentils (masoor dal), rinsed

175 g/6 oz new potatoes, scrubbed and finely diced

1 large carrot, finely diced

1 green pepper, deseeded and finely chopped

1 litre/1¾ pints cold water

¼ tsp ground turmeric

¼ tsp asafoetida

1 tbsp tamarind paste

2 tsp sambhar masala, or to taste (see page 29)

salt

GARNISH

1½ tbsp vegetable or groundnut oil

12 fresh curry leaves

2 dried red chillies

1 tsp black mustard seeds

1 Put the red lentils in a bowl with enough water to cover and leave to soak for 30 minutes, changing the water once.

2 Drain the lentils. Put them in a wok or large frying pan with the potatoes, carrot and green pepper and pour over the water. Bring to the boil, skimming the surface as necessary. Reduce the heat to the lowest setting, stir in the turmeric and asafoetida and partially cover the pan. Simmer, stirring occasionally, for 15–20 minutes, until the vegetables and lentils are tender but the lentils aren't falling apart.

3 Stir in the tamarind paste and sambhar masala. Taste and adjust the seasoning, adding extra masala and salt to taste. Continue simmering slowly while making the garnish.

4 To make the garnish, heat the oil in a large pan over a high heat. Add the curry leaves, chillies and mustard seeds and stir around quickly, taking care to stand back because they will splutter. Transfer the lentil mixture to a serving dish and pour over the hot oil and spices. Serve immediately.

Mattar paneer

PEAS & PANEER IN CHILLI-TOMATO SAUCE

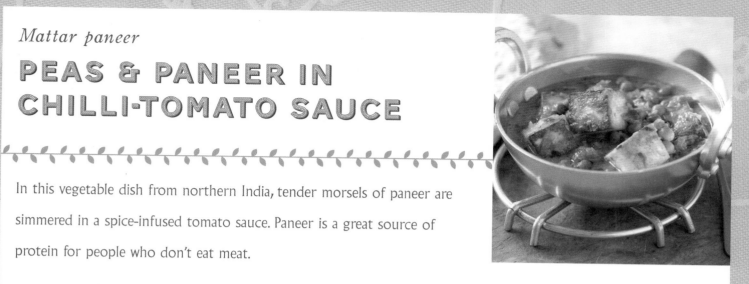

In this vegetable dish from northern India, tender morsels of paneer are simmered in a spice-infused tomato sauce. Paneer is a great source of protein for people who don't eat meat.

SERVES: 4

PREP: 10–15 minutes

COOK: 30–35 minutes

4 tbsp vegetable or groundnut oil

250 g/9 oz paneer, cut into 2.5-cm/1-inch cubes

4 green cardamom pods, bruised

2 bay leaves

1 onion, finely chopped

2 tsp garlic paste

2 tsp ginger paste

2 tsp ground coriander

½ tsp ground turmeric

½–1 tsp chilli powder

150 g/5½ oz canned chopped tomatoes

450 ml/16 fl oz warm water

1 tsp salt, or to taste

125 g/4½ oz frozen peas

½ tsp garam masala

2 tbsp single cream

2 tbsp chopped fresh coriander

1 Heat 2 tablespoons of the oil in a non-stick saucepan over a medium heat. Add the paneer and cook, stirring frequently, for 3–4 minutes, or until evenly browned. Remove the paneer from the pan and drain on kitchen paper. Set aside.

2 Add the remaining oil to the pan and reduce the heat to low. Add the cardamom pods and bay leaves and leave to sizzle gently for 20–25 seconds. Add the onion, increase the heat to medium and cook, stirring frequently, for 4–5 minutes, until the onion is soft. Add the garlic and ginger pastes and cook, stirring frequently, until the onion is a pale golden colour.

3 Add the ground coriander, turmeric and chilli powder and cook, stirring, for 1 minute. Add the tomatoes and cook, stirring, for 4–5 minutes. Add 2 tablespoons of the water and cook, stirring, for 3 minutes, or until the oil separates from the spice paste.

4 Add the remaining water and the salt. Bring to the boil, then simmer, uncovered, for 7–8 minutes. Add the reserved paneer and the peas and simmer for 5 minutes. Stir in the garam masala, cream and chopped coriander, then remove from the heat. Serve immediately.

Aloo gobhi

GARLIC & CHILLI-FLAVOURED POTATOES WITH CAULIFLOWER

This well-known and popular Indian dish always contains potatoes and cauliflower but other ingredients can vary — there are as many different versions as there are cooks! This recipe is easy to make, can be part-prepared ahead (up to step 2) and tastes delicious.

SERVES: 4

PREP: 10 minutes, plus soaking time

COOK: 30 minutes

350 g/12 oz new potatoes

1 small cauliflower

2 tbsp vegetable or groundnut oil

1 tsp black or brown mustard seeds

1 tsp cumin seeds

5 large garlic cloves, lightly crushed, then chopped

1–2 fresh green chillies, finely chopped (deseeded if you like)

½ tsp ground turmeric

½ tsp salt, or to taste

2 tbsp chopped fresh coriander

1 Cook the potatoes in their skins in a saucepan of boiling water for 20 minutes, or until tender. Drain, then soak in cold water for 30 minutes. Peel them, if you like, then halve or quarter according to their size — they should be only slightly bigger than the size of the cauliflower florets.

2 Meanwhile, divide the cauliflower into small florets and blanch in a large saucepan of boiling salted water for 3 minutes. Drain and plunge into iced water to prevent further cooking, then drain again.

3 Heat the oil in a saucepan over a medium heat. When hot, but not smoking, add the mustard seeds, then the cumin seeds. Remove from the heat and add the garlic and chillies. Return to a low heat and cook, stirring, until the garlic has a light brown tinge.

4 Stir in the turmeric, followed by the cauliflower and the potatoes. Add the salt, increase the heat slightly and cook, stirring, until the vegetables are well blended with the spices and heated through.

5 Stir in the chopped coriander, remove from the heat and serve immediately.

Baingan ka bharta

SPICED AUBERGINE MASH

The word *bharta* (pronounced 'bhurr-taaah') refers to dishes in which the ingredients are roughly mashed either before or after the dish is prepared. Bhartas are largely north Indian in origin and can be made from all sorts of vegetables. This version of *baingan ka bharta* has its origins in the Punjab.

SERVES: 4

PREP: 15–20 minutes

COOK: 45–55 minutes

4 large aubergines
2 tbsp vegetable or groundnut oil
55 g/2 oz butter
2 onions, finely chopped
2 tsp grated fresh ginger
4 garlic cloves, crushed
2 fresh green chillies, finely sliced
3 tomatoes, finely chopped
2 tsp salt
1 tsp chilli powder
1 tsp smoked paprika
2 tsp ground coriander
1 tsp ground cumin
1 tsp ground turmeric
½ tsp garam masala
6 tbsp finely chopped fresh coriander

1 Prick the aubergines all over with a fork and roast them over an open flame (if you have a gas hob) or under a medium–hot grill, turning them from time to time, for 20–25 minutes, until the skin blackens and chars. To check if the aubergines are cooked, press the back of a spoon into the skin – if it enters the aubergine like soft butter, it is done. Allow to cool.

2 When the aubergines are cool enough to handle, remove the skins and roughly mash the pulp. Set aside.

3 Heat the oil and butter in a large, non-stick frying pan and add the onions. Sauté for 5–6 minutes, until softened. Add the ginger, garlic and chillies and stir-fry for 1–2 minutes.

4 Stir in the tomatoes and salt and cook for 12–15 minutes. Add the chilli powder, paprika, ground coriander, ground cumin and turmeric.

5 Stir in the reserved aubergine flesh and cook for about 3–4 minutes. Stir in the garam masala and chopped coriander. Serve immediately.

TIP

If cooking the aubergines on the hob, it is a good idea to line the base of the hob with aluminium foil to make it easy to clean later.

Mumbai aloo

BOMBAY POTATOES

This simple dish of spiced potatoes is easy to make and goes with almost anything. Any leftovers can be wrapped up in a chapatti for a quick lunch or snack the next day.

SERVES: 6

PREP: 10 minutes

COOK: 30 minutes

500 g/1 lb 2 oz new potatoes, halved

1 tsp ground turmeric

pinch of salt

55 g/2 oz ghee or 4 tbsp vegetable or groundnut oil

6 fresh curry leaves

1 dried red chilli

2 fresh green chillies, chopped

½ tsp nigella seeds

1 tsp black mustard seeds

½ tsp cumin seeds

½ tsp fennel seeds

¼ tsp asafoetida

2 onions, chopped

5 tbsp chopped fresh coriander

juice of ½ lime

1 Place the potatoes in a large, heavy-based saucepan and pour in just enough cold water to cover. Add ½ teaspoon of the turmeric and the salt and bring to the boil. Simmer for 10 minutes, or until tender. Drain and set aside.

2 Heat the ghee in a large, heavy-based frying pan. Add the curry leaves and dried red chilli and cook, stirring frequently, for a few minutes, or until the chilli is blackened.

3 Add the remaining turmeric, the green chillies, nigella seeds, mustard seeds, cumin seeds, fennel seeds, asafoetida, onions and chopped coriander. Cook, stirring constantly, for 5 minutes, or until the onions have softened.

4 Stir in the reserved potatoes and cook over a low heat, stirring frequently, for 10 minutes, or until heated through. Squeeze over the lime juice and serve immediately.

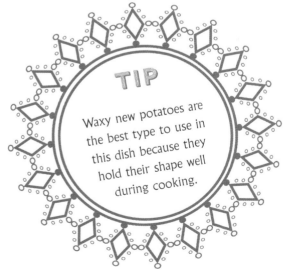

TIP

Waxy new potatoes are the best type to use in this dish because they hold their shape well during cooking.

Bhindi-pyaaz

OKRA STIR-FRIED WITH ONIONS

Bhindi, or okra, is a versatile vegetable. The combination of the soft green okra, bright red pepper and white onion in this dish, all dotted with dark mustard seeds, creates a feast for the eyes.

SERVES: 4

PREP: 15 minutes

COOK: 10 minutes

280 g/10 oz okra

1 small red pepper

1 onion

2 tbsp vegetable or groundnut oil

1 tsp black or brown mustard seeds

½ tsp cumin seeds

3 large garlic cloves, lightly crushed, then chopped

½ tsp chilli powder

½ tsp salt, or to taste

½ tsp garam masala

1 Scrub each okra gently, rinse well in cold running water, then slice off the hard head. Halve diagonally and set aside.

2 Remove the seeds and core from the red pepper and cut into 4-cm/1½-inch strips. Halve the onion lengthways and cut into 5 mm/¼ inch thick slices. Set aside.

3 Heat the oil in a heavy-based frying pan or wok over a medium heat. When hot, but not smoking, add the mustard seeds, followed by the cumin seeds. Remove from the heat and add the garlic. Return to a low heat and cook the garlic gently, stirring, for 1 minute, or until lightly browned.

4 Add the reserved okra, red pepper and onion, increase the heat to medium—high and stir-fry for 2 minutes. Add the chilli powder and salt and stir-fry for a further 3 minutes. Add the garam masala and stir-fry for 1 minute. Remove from the heat and serve immediately.

TIP

To test the oil temperature in step 3, drop in a couple of mustard seeds – they should pop straightaway.

Bharwan baigan tamattari

TOMATO-STUFFED AUBERGINES

From Maharashtra, this is a technique for cooking whole, small aubergines with a thin layer of spicy stuffing between the slices. It is an excellent dish for entertaining because the fiddly work can be done well in advance.

MAKES: 4

PREP: 20–30 minutes

COOK: 30–35 minutes

4 small aubergines, about 13 cm/
5 inches long

vegetable or groundnut oil,
for shallow-frying

STUFFING

4 firm tomatoes, grated

2 onions, grated

2 fresh red chillies, chopped
(deseeded if you like)

4 tbsp lemon juice

4 tbsp finely chopped fresh coriander

½ tbsp garlic paste

½ tbsp ginger paste

1½ tbsp ground coriander

2 tsp ground cumin

1 tsp fennel seeds

1 tsp ground turmeric

1 tsp salt

1 tbsp gram flour (if needed)

1 To make the stuffing, mix together the tomatoes, onions, chillies, lemon juice, chopped coriander, garlic paste, ginger paste, ground coriander, ground cumin, fennel seeds, turmeric and salt in a non-metallic bowl. The filling should not be stiff, but thick enough that it doesn't slide off the aubergine slices. If the tomatoes are very juicy and have made the filling too runny, gradually stir in the gram flour.

2 To prepare the aubergines, work with one at a time. Slit lengthways into four parallel slices, without cutting through the stem end, so that the aubergine remains in one piece. Lightly fan the slices apart, then use a small spoon or your fingers to fill, dividing a quarter of the stuffing between the slices and covering each slice to the edges. Carefully layer the slices back into position so the aubergine looks whole again. Repeat this process with the remaining aubergines.

3 Choose a heavy-based frying pan with a tight-fitting lid – it needs to be large enough to hold the aubergines in a single layer. Heat enough oil to cover the base of the pan with a layer about 5 mm/¼ inch deep, then add the aubergines in a single layer.

4 Put the pan over the lowest heat and cover tightly. Leave to cook for 15 minutes, then carefully turn the aubergines over. Re-cover the pan and continue cooking for a further 10–15 minutes, or until the aubergines are tender when you pierce them with a skewer or a knife. Check occasionally while the aubergines are cooking and, if they start to stick to the base of the pan, stir in a couple of tablespoons of water. Serve hot or at room temperature.

Tandoori khumbi

TANDOORI MUSHROOM CURRY

This north Indian mushroom curry makes for great vegetarian entertaining. If you like, you can replace the peas with chopped spinach leaves for a tasty variation. Serve hot with cooked basmati rice or warm chapattis.

SERVES: 4

PREP: 15–20 minutes

COOK: 35 minutes

2 tbsp vegetable or groundnut oil

1 tsp cumin seeds

1 tsp coriander seeds

1 onion, finely chopped

2 tsp ground coriander

1 tsp ground cumin

6 black peppercorns

½ tsp freshly ground cardamom seeds

1 tsp ground turmeric

1 tbsp tandoori masala (see page 29)

1 fresh red chilli, finely chopped

2 garlic cloves, crushed

2 tsp grated fresh ginger

800 g/1 lb 12 oz canned chopped tomatoes

600 g/1 lb 5 oz chestnut or button mushrooms, halved or thickly sliced

2 tsp salt

200 g/7 oz fresh or frozen peas

4 tbsp roughly chopped fresh coriander

6 tbsp single cream

1 Heat the oil in a large saucepan over a medium heat. Add the cumin seeds and coriander seeds and cook for 1 minute, or until sizzling.

2 Add the onion, ground coriander, cumin, peppercorns, ground cardamom seeds, turmeric, tandoori masala, chilli, garlic and ginger. Cook, stirring, for 2–3 minutes, or until onion is soft and the mixture is aromatic.

3 Add the tomatoes, mushrooms and salt. Stir until well combined. Bring to the boil, then reduce the heat to low and cook, uncovered, for 25 minutes.

4 Add the peas and stir to mix well. Cook for a further 4–5 minutes, or until piping hot.

5 Remove from the heat, scatter over the coriander and drizzle over the cream. Stir to mix well. Serve immediately.

Patrani macchi

PARSI-STYLE BAKED FISH WRAPPED IN BANANA LEAVES

This delicious Parsi-style baked fish dish, from the western shores of India, looks very pretty when served wrapped up in banana leaves. Your guests will enjoy the mouth-watering aromas that are released as they unwrap their individual packages at the table.

SERVES: 4

PREP: 15–20 minutes

COOK: 15–20 minutes

4 thick cod fillets, about 200 g/7 oz each, skinned

2 tsp ground turmeric

1 large fresh banana leaf

SPICE PASTE

2 tsp ground cumin

2 tsp ground coriander

1½ tsp palm sugar

200 ml/7 fl oz coconut cream

4 fresh red chillies, deseeded and chopped

100 g/3½ oz chopped fresh coriander

4 tbsp chopped fresh mint

5 garlic cloves, chopped

1 tsp finely grated fresh ginger

4 tbsp vegetable or groundnut oil

juice of 2 limes

2 tsp salt

1 Preheat the oven to 200°C/400°F/ Gas Mark 6.

2 Place the fish fillets in a single layer on a plate and sprinkle over the turmeric. Rub into the fish and set aside.

3 Place the ingredients for the spice paste in a food processer and blend until fairly smooth. Set aside.

4 Cut the banana leaf into four 24-cm/9½-inch squares. Soften the banana leaf squares by dipping them into a pan of very hot water for a few seconds. Once the banana leaf squares have become pliant, wipe them dry with kitchen paper and arrange on a work surface.

5 Apply the spice paste liberally to both sides of each piece of fish. Place a piece of fish on top of each banana leaf square and wrap up like a parcel, securing with bamboo skewers or string.

6 Place the parcels on a baking tray and bake in the preheated oven for 15–20 minutes, until cooked through. Transfer to plates and serve immediately.

TIP

Fresh banana leaves are available from Asian grocery stores. If you can't get hold of any, use squares of lightly oiled aluminium foil instead.

Kaalvan

MAHARASHTRIAN SALMON CURRY

This simple fish curry is packed with flavour. *Kaalvan* is the Maharashtrian term for any sauce-based fish dish. You can use any firm fish fillet or fish steaks instead of the salmon, if desired. Serve with freshly cooked basmati rice to soak up the delicious cooking liquid.

SERVES: 4

PREP: 5–10 minutes

COOK: 15–20 minutes

6 tbsp vegetable or groundnut oil

8 salmon steaks, each about 150 g/5½ oz

2 tsp cornflour

1 tsp hot chilli powder

1 tsp paprika

½ tsp ground turmeric

2 tsp ground cumin

1 tsp ground coriander

2 tsp salt

1 tsp tamarind paste

400 ml/14 fl oz coconut milk

400 ml/14 fl oz cold water

1 Heat the oil in a non-stick saucepan and add the fish. Fry the salmon for 1–2 minutes on each side.

2 Mix together the cornflour, spices, salt, tamarind paste and coconut milk. Pour this mixture into the saucepan with the water.

3 Bring to the boil, then reduce the heat, cover and cook gently for 10–12 minutes, or until the fish is cooked through and the sauce has thickened slightly (it should still be quite runny). Serve immediately.

Goa che nalla chi kadi

GOAN-STYLE SEAFOOD CURRY

With mustard seeds, curry leaves and a creamy coconut sauce, this quick and easy dish could have originated anywhere in southern India, not just in tropical Goa on the west coast.

SERVES: 4–6

PREP: 15 minutes

COOK: 20 minutes

3 tbsp vegetable or groundnut oil

1 tbsp black mustard seeds

12 fresh curry leaves

6 shallots, finely chopped

1 garlic clove, crushed

1 tsp ground turmeric

½ tsp ground coriander

¼–½ tsp chilli powder

140 g/5 oz creamed coconut, grated and dissolved in 300 ml/10 fl oz boiling water

500 g/1 lb 2 oz skinless, boneless white fish, such as monkfish or cod, cut into large chunks

450 g/1 lb large raw prawns, peeled and deveined

juice and finely grated rind of 1 lime

salt

1. Heat the oil in a wok or large frying pan over a high heat. Add the mustard seeds and stir them around for about 1 minute, or until they start to pop. Stir in the curry leaves.

2. Add the shallots and garlic and stir-fry for about 5 minutes, or until the shallots are golden. Stir in the turmeric, ground coriander and chilli powder and continue stir-frying for about 30 seconds. Add the dissolved creamed coconut. Bring to the boil, then reduce the heat to medium and stir for about 2 minutes.

3. Reduce the heat to low, add the fish and simmer for 1 minute, spooning the sauce over the fish and very gently stirring it around. Add the prawns and continue to simmer for a further 4–5 minutes, until the fish flakes easily and the prawns curl and turn pink.

4. Add half the lime juice, then taste and add more lime juice and salt if needed. Sprinkle with the lime rind and serve immediately.

TIP

Creamed coconut is available as pressed white bars — you simply grate off the amount you need.

Macchi masala

BALTI FISH CURRY

This dish is one for those who prefer robustly flavoured dishes, like the ones served in northern India, to the coconut-based ones of the south. It is particularly tasty when served with any Indian bread.

SERVES: 4–6

PREP: 10–15 minutes, plus marinating time

COOK: 15–20 minutes

900 g/2 lb thick white fish fillets, such as monkfish, cod or haddock, cut into large chunks

140 g/5 oz ghee or 150 ml/5 fl oz vegetable or groundnut oil

2 large onions, chopped

½ tbsp salt

150 ml/5 fl oz cold water

chopped fresh coriander, to garnish

MARINADE

¾ tsp garlic paste

¾ tsp ginger paste

1 fresh green chilli, deseeded and chopped

1 tsp ground coriander

1 tsp ground cumin

½ tsp ground turmeric

¼–½ tsp chilli powder

pinch of salt

1 tbsp cold water

2 bay leaves, torn

1 To make the marinade, mix together the garlic and ginger pastes, green chilli, ground coriander, cumin, turmeric, chilli powder and salt in a large bowl. Gradually stir in the water to form a thin paste.

2 Add the fish chunks to the marinade and toss gently to coat with the spice mixture. Tuck the bay leaves underneath and leave to marinate in the refrigerator for at least 30 minutes, or up to 4 hours.

3 Remove the fish from the refrigerator 15 minutes in advance of cooking. Melt the ghee in a large frying pan or wok over a medium–high heat. Add the onions, sprinkle with the salt and cook, stirring frequently, for 8 minutes, or until they are very soft and golden.

4 Gently add the fish with its marinade to the pan and stir in the water. Bring to the boil, then immediately reduce the heat and cook, spooning the sauce over the fish and stirring gently, for 4–5 minutes, until the fish is cooked through and the flesh flakes easily. Garnish with chopped coriander and serve immediately.

Doi mach

SOLE IN CHILLI YOGURT

This dish is typical of the cuisine of the Bengal region, where seafood is an important part of the everyday diet. It can also be made using butter fish, one of the jewels of Indian seafood cooking, or flounder. Freshly cooked okra would make a delicious accompaniment.

SERVES: 4

PREP: 15–20 minutes

COOK: 20–25 minutes

2 tbsp vegetable or groundnut oil

1 large onion, sliced

4-cm/1½-inch piece fresh ginger, finely chopped

½ tsp salt

¼ tsp ground turmeric

pinch of ground cinnamon

pinch of ground cloves

200 g/7 oz wholemilk natural yogurt

1 tbsp plain flour

small pinch of chilli powder

4 skinless sole fillets, about 150 g/5½ oz each, wiped dry

30 g/1 oz ghee or 2 tbsp vegetable or groundnut oil

salt and pepper

sliced fresh green chillies, to garnish

1 Heat the oil in a large frying pan over a medium–high heat. Add the onion and stir-fry for 8 minutes, or until it is soft and dark golden brown. Add the ginger and stir around for a further minute.

2 Add the salt, turmeric, cinnamon and cloves and stir-fry for a further 30 seconds. Remove the pan from the heat and stir in the yogurt, a little at a time, beating constantly.

3 Transfer the yogurt mixture to a blender or food processor and process until a paste forms.

4 Season the flour with the chilli powder and salt and pepper to taste. Spread out the seasoned flour on a plate and use to dust the fish fillets lightly on both sides.

5 Wipe out the frying pan with kitchen paper, then melt the ghee over a medium–high heat. When it is bubbling, reduce the heat to medium and add the fish fillets in a single layer. Cook for 2½ minutes, or until golden.

6 Turn over the fish fillets and continue cooking for a further minute. Add the yogurt sauce to the pan and reheat, stirring, until the sauce is hot, the fish is cooked through and the flesh flakes easily. Transfer to plates, garnish with green chilli and serve immediately.

Macher jhol

BENGALI FISH CURRY

Cooking with highly flavoured mustard oil, as in this dish, is very common in the Bengal region. Heating mustard oil to smoking point, then allowing it to cool before cooking reduces the pungent smell and taste of the oil. You can, however, use vegetable or groundnut oil if you prefer a milder flavour.

SERVES: 4

PREP: 15 minutes

COOK: 25–30 minutes

2 tsp coriander seeds

1 tsp cumin seeds

4 tbsp mustard oil

800 g/1 lb 12 oz monkfish fillets, cut into large, bite-sized pieces

2 potatoes, cut into finger-thick batons

1 tsp ground turmeric

2 tsp salt

5 fresh green chillies, slit lengthways

1 tbsp panch phoran

800 ml/1⅓ pints cold water

cooked basmati rice, to serve

1 Dry-fry the coriander seeds and cumin seeds in a small frying pan for 1–2 minutes. Tip the seeds out of the pan and leave to cool, then finely grind in a spice grinder (or use a mortar and pestle). Set aside.

2 Heat 2 tablespoons of the mustard oil in a heavy-based saucepan until it just reaches smoking point. Remove from the heat and allow to cool, then heat up the oil again over a medium heat. Add the fish and fry for a minute on each side. Remove with a slotted spoon and set aside.

3 Heat the remaining oil in the pan, add the potatoes and stir-fry for 2–3 minutes. Add the turmeric, salt, chillies, panch phoran and the reserved ground spices and stir-fry for 1 minute.

4 Pour in the water and bring to the boil. Reduce the heat and simmer for 12–15 minutes, or until the potatoes are just tender. Add the fish into the saucepan and simmer for 3–4 minutes, or until the fish is cooked through and the flesh flakes easily. Serve immediately with cooked basmati rice.

Paatrani macchi

STEAMED FISH WITH CORIANDER CHUTNEY

South Indian food is often served on glossy, dark-green banana leaves. Here the leaves are wrapped around fish fillets with a fresh-tasting chutney to keep the fish moist while it cooks.

SERVES: 4

PREP: 10–15 minutes

COOK: 15 minutes

1 large fresh banana leaf

vegetable or groundnut oil, for brushing

4 white fish fillets, such as pomfret or sole, about 140 g/5 oz each

225 g/8 oz coriander chutney (see page 40)

salt and pepper

lemon wedges, to serve

1 Cut the banana leaf into four squares, each large enough to fold around a fish fillet to make a tight parcel. Working with one banana leaf square at a time, very lightly brush one side with oil. Put one of the fish fillets in the centre of the oiled side, flesh-side up. Spread one quarter of the coriander chutney over the top and season to taste with salt and pepper.

2 Wrap up the banana leaf square like a parcel, securing with bamboo skewers or string. Repeat with the remaining ingredients and banana leaf squares.

3 Place a steamer large enough to hold the parcels in a single layer over a pan of boiling water. Add the fish, cover the pan and steam for 15 minutes, or until the fish is cooked through and the flesh flakes easily. Transfer the fish parcels to plates and serve with lemon wedges for squeezing over.

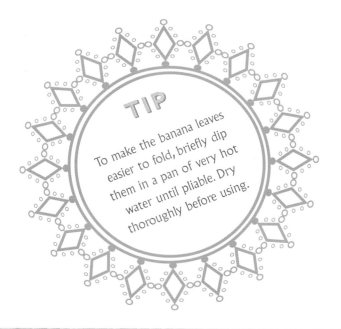

TIP

To make the banana leaves easier to fold, briefly dip them in a pan of very hot water until pliable. Dry thoroughly before using.

Tissario kadugu

MUSSELS WITH MUSTARD SEEDS & SHALLOTS

Baskets piled high with fresh mussels are a common sight along India's southern Malabar coast and quickly cooked, fragrant dishes like this are typical of those served in the local open-air harbourside restaurants.

SERVES: 4   **PREP:** 5–10 minutes   **COOK:** 10–12 minutes

2 kg / 4 lb 8 oz live mussels, scrubbed and debearded

3 tbsp vegetable or groundnut oil

½ tbsp black mustard seeds

8 shallots, chopped

2 garlic cloves, crushed

2 tbsp white wine vinegar

4 small fresh red chillies

85 g / 3 oz creamed coconut, grated and dissolved in 300 ml / 10 fl oz boiling water

10 fresh curry leaves

½ tsp ground turmeric

¼–½ tsp chilli powder

pinch of salt, or to taste

1 Discard any mussels with broken shells and any that refuse to close when tapped with a knife. Set the remainder aside.

2 Heat the oil in a large frying pan or wok over a medium–high heat. Add the mustard seeds and stir them around for about 1 minute, or until they start to pop.

3 Add the shallots and garlic and cook, stirring frequently, for 3 minutes, or until they start to brown. Stir in the vinegar, whole chillies, dissolved creamed coconut, curry leaves, turmeric, chilli powder and salt and bring to the boil, stirring.

4 Reduce the heat to very low. Add the reserved mussels, cover the pan and leave to simmer, shaking the pan frequently, for 3–4 minutes, or until they are all open. Discard any mussels that remain closed. Ladle the mussels into deep bowls, then taste the broth and adjust the seasoning, adding extra salt if needed. Spoon the broth over the mussels and serve immediately.

TIP

If the mussels were gritty, strain the broth through a muslin-lined sieve.

Meen moilee

SOUTH INDIAN COCONUT FISH CURRY

This lightly spiced fish and coconut dish from the coastal region of Kerala combines fresh ingredients in a simple but effective way. It is a prime example of India's minimalist cooking with maximum flavour. Serve with freshly cooked basmati rice.

SERVES: 4

PREP: 10 minutes

COOK: 30–35 minutes

2 tsp salt

2 tsp ground turmeric

4 halibut fillets or steaks, each about 200 g/7 oz

2 tbsp vegetable or groundnut oil

2 onions, finely sliced

4 fresh green chillies, slit lengthways

3 garlic cloves, very thinly sliced

12 fresh curry leaves

400 ml/14 fl oz coconut milk

4 tbsp finely chopped fresh coriander

1 Mix a teaspoon of the salt with a teaspoon of the turmeric. Gently rub into the fish fillets and set aside for 10–12 minutes.

2 Meanwhile, heat the oil in a frying pan. Add the onions, chillies and garlic and stir-fry for a few minutes. Add the curry leaves and continue to cook over a low–medium heat for 12–15 minutes, or until the onion is translucent.

3 Add the remaining turmeric and salt to the pan. Pour in the coconut milk and bring to a simmer.

4 Add the fish, in a single layer, and simmer very gently for 5–6 minutes, or until just cooked through.

5 Remove from the heat and scatter over the chopped coriander. Serve immediately.

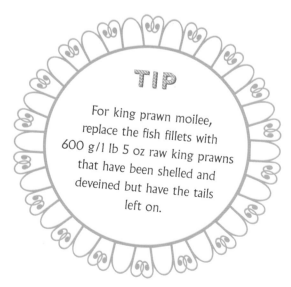

TIP

For king prawn moilee, replace the fish fillets with 600 g/1 lb 5 oz raw king prawns that have been shelled and deveined but have the tails left on.

Tamatar macchi

FISH IN TOMATO & CHILLI SAUCE WITH FRIED ONION

This delicious dish, in which firm-fleshed fish is shallow-fried until browned and then simmered in an alluringly spiced chilli and tomato sauce, originates from north-east India. It is best served with freshly cooked basmati rice and poppadoms.

SERVES: 4

PREP: 10 minutes, plus marinating time

COOK: 35–40 minutes

700 g/1 lb 9 oz white fish fillets, such as sole, cod or haddock, cut into 5-cm/2-inch pieces

2 tbsp lemon juice

1 tsp salt, or to taste

1 tsp ground turmeric

4 tbsp vegetable or groundnut oil, plus extra for shallow-frying

2 tsp sugar

1 large onion, finely chopped

2 tsp ginger paste

2 tsp garlic paste

½ tsp ground fennel seeds

1 tsp ground coriander

½–1 tsp chilli powder

175 g/6 oz canned chopped tomatoes

300 ml/10 fl oz warm water

2–3 tbsp chopped fresh coriander

1 Place the fish on a large plate and gently rub in the lemon juice, ½ teaspoon of the salt and ½ teaspoon of the turmeric. Set aside for 15–20 minutes.

2 Pour enough oil into a frying pan to fill to a depth of about 1 cm/½ inch and place over a medium–high heat. When the oil is hot, fry the pieces of fish, in a single layer, until well browned on both sides and a light crust is formed. Drain on kitchen paper.

3 Heat the 4 tablespoons of oil in a saucepan or frying pan over a medium heat and add the sugar. Allow it to brown, watching it carefully because once it browns it will blacken quickly. As soon as the sugar is brown, add the onion and cook for 5 minutes, until soft. Add the ginger and garlic pastes and cook for a further 3–4 minutes, or until the mixture begins to brown.

4 Add the ground fennel seeds, ground coriander, chilli powder and the remaining turmeric. Cook for about a minute, then add half the tomatoes. Stir and cook until the tomato juice has evaporated, then add the remaining tomatoes. Continue to cook, stirring, until the oil separates from the spice paste.

5 Pour in the water and add the remaining salt. Bring to the boil and reduce the heat to medium. Add the fish, stir gently and reduce the heat to low. Cook, uncovered, for 5–6 minutes, then stir in half the chopped coriander and remove from the heat. Garnish with the remaining coriander and serve immediately.

Murgh chettinad

PEPPERED SOUTH INDIAN CHICKEN CURRY

This dish originates from Chettinad, which is a region in the state of Tamil Nadu in the most southerly tip of India. Chettinad is well known for its many temples and its delicious cuisine. The latter tends to be on the hot and spicy side, so it is not for the faint-hearted!

SERVES: 4

PREP: 25 minutes

COOK: 30 minutes

4 tbsp vegetable or groundnut oil

1 tsp black mustard seeds

pinch of asafoetida

8–10 fresh curry leaves

600 g/1 lb 5 oz skinless, boneless chicken thighs, cut into large bite-sized pieces

2 tsp ground cumin

1 tsp ground coriander

1 tsp ground turmeric

2 tsp salt

2 tbsp pepper

1 tsp chilli powder

200 ml/7 fl oz coconut cream

200 ml/7 fl oz cold water

1 tsp finely grated fresh ginger

juice of 1 lime

6 tbsp finely chopped fresh coriander

1 Heat the oil in a non-stick saucepan over a medium heat. Add the mustard seeds and, when they start to pop, add the asafoetida and curry leaves and stir-fry for 30 seconds.

2 Add the chicken and stir-fry for 4–5 minutes. Add the cumin, ground coriander, turmeric, salt, pepper and chilli powder and stir-fry for 1–2 minutes.

3 Add in the coconut cream and water, stir to mix well and cook over a low–medium heat for 15–20 minutes, or until the chicken is cooked through.

4 Stir in the ginger, then remove the pan from the heat and stir in the lime juice. Scatter over the chopped coriander and serve immediately.

TIP

Coconut cream is richer and thicker than coconut milk with a higher ratio of coconut to water. It is available ready-made in cans or cartons.

Murgh nu farcha

PARSI-STYLE FRIED CHICKEN

In this Parsi-style chicken recipe, chicken pieces are marinated in spices, crumbed and fried until crisp and golden. For a variation, use turkey breast fillets instead of the chicken and cut them into finger-thick strips. This dish is delicious served warm.

SERVES: 4

PREP: 15–20 minutes, plus marinating time

COOK: 10–18 minutes

1 tsp chilli powder

1 fresh green chilli, finely chopped

2 tsp salt

1 tsp ground cumin

1 tsp ground coriander

2 tsp grated fresh ginger

3 garlic cloves, crushed

1 tbsp white wine vinegar

1 tsp palm sugar

4 tbsp finely chopped fresh coriander

600 g/1 lb 5 oz skinless, boneless chicken breasts, cut into bite-sized pieces

3 eggs

100 g/3½ oz dried white breadcrumbs

vegetable or groundnut oil, for deep-frying

1 Place the chilli powder, green chilli, salt, cumin, ground coriander, ginger, garlic, vinegar, palm sugar and chopped coriander in a mixing bowl. Add the chicken and stir to mix well. Cover and leave to marinate in the refrigerator for 6–8 hours, or overnight if possible.

2 Beat the eggs in a shallow bowl. Spread out the breadcrumbs on a large plate. Dip the chicken pieces in the beaten egg, then roll in the breadcrumbs to coat evenly, shaking off the excess.

3 Heat enough oil for deep-frying in a large saucepan or deep-fryer to 180–190°C/350–375°F, or until a cube of bread browns in 30 seconds. Deep-fry the chicken pieces, in batches, for 5–6 minutes, or until crisp, golden and cooked through. Remove with a slotted spoon and drain on kitchen paper. Serve warm.

Tandoori murgh

TANDOORI CHICKEN

This recipe would traditionally be cooked in a tandoor oven — a simple, conical clay oven that is heated by glowing charcoals or wood in its base. For the best flavour, allow the chicken to marinate for a day before cooking.

SERVES: 4

1 chicken, weighing 1.5 kg/3 lb 5 oz, skinned

½ lemon

1 tsp salt

30 g/1 oz ghee, melted

fresh coriander sprigs, to garnish

lemon wedges, to serve

TANDOORI PASTE

½ tbsp garlic paste

½ tbsp ginger paste

1 tbsp ground paprika

1 tsp ground cinnamon

1 tsp ground cumin

½ tsp ground coriander

¼ tsp chilli powder, ideally Kashmiri chilli powder

pinch of ground cloves

¼ tsp red food colouring (optional)

a few drops of yellow food colouring (optional)

200 g/7 oz wholemilk natural yogurt

PREP: 5–10 minutes, plus marinating time

1. To make the tandoori paste, combine the garlic and ginger pastes, dry spices and food colouring (if using) in a bowl and stir in the yogurt. You can use the paste now or store it in an airtight container in the refrigerator for up to 3 days.

2. Use a small knife to make slashes all over the chicken. Rub the lemon half over the chicken, then rub the salt into the slashes. Put the chicken in a deep bowl, add the tandoori paste and use your hands to rub it all over the chicken and into the slashes. Cover the bowl with clingfilm and chill in the refrigerator for at least 4 hours, but ideally up to 24 hours.

3. Just before you are ready to cook, preheat the oven to 200°C/400°F/ Gas Mark 6. Put the chicken on a rack in a roasting tin, breast-side up, and drizzle over the melted ghee. Roast in the preheated oven for 45 minutes, then quickly remove the bird and roasting tin from the oven and turn the temperature to its highest setting.

COOK: 55 minutes–1 hour, plus standing time

4. Very carefully pour out any fat from the bottom of the roasting tin. Return the chicken to the oven and roast for a further 10–15 minutes, until the chicken is tender and the juices run clear when a skewer is inserted into the thickest part of the meat and the paste is lightly charred.

5. Leave to stand for 10 minutes, then cut into pieces. Garnish with coriander sprigs and serve with lemon wedges.

Murgh makhani

BUTTER CHICKEN

The quickest way to prepare this popular Sikh dish is to buy a ready-cooked tandoori chicken. Otherwise, start with the tandoori chicken recipe on the opposite page.

SERVES: 4–6

PREP: 5–10 minutes

COOK: 25 minutes

1 onion, chopped

2 tsp garlic paste

2 tsp ginger paste

400 g/14 oz canned chopped tomatoes

¼–½ tsp chilli powder

pinch of sugar

pinch of salt

30 g/1 oz ghee or 2 tbsp vegetable or groundnut oil

125 ml/4 fl oz cold water

1 tbsp tomato purée

40 g/1½ oz butter, cut into small pieces

½ tsp garam masala

½ tsp ground cumin

½ tsp ground coriander

1 cooked tandoori chicken, cut into 8 pieces

4 tbsp double cream

chopped cashew nuts and fresh coriander sprigs, to garnish

1 Put the onion, garlic paste and ginger paste in a food processor or blender and process until a paste forms. Add the tomatoes, chilli powder, sugar and salt and process again until blended.

2 Melt the ghee in a large frying pan or wok over a medium–high heat. Add the onion and tomato mixture and the water and stir in the tomato purée.

3 Bring the mixture to the boil, stirring, then reduce the heat to very low and simmer for 5 minutes, stirring occasionally, until the sauce thickens.

4 Stir in half the butter, the garam masala, cumin and ground coriander. Add the chicken pieces and stir around until they are well coated. Simmer for about 10 minutes, or until the chicken is warmed through.

5 Lightly beat the cream in a small bowl and stir in several tablespoons of the hot sauce, beating constantly. Stir the cream mixture into the pan, then add the remaining butter and stir until it melts. Garnish with chopped cashew nuts and coriander sprigs and serve immediately.

Murgh biryani

CHICKEN BIRYANI

In this dish from the snowy foothills of the Himalayas, the naturally fragrant basmati rice is enhanced with cinnamon, cardamom and star anise and layered with delicately spiced chicken. It is cooked in a sealed pot to conserve the flavours.

SERVES: 4

PREP: 15 minutes, plus marinating & infusing time

COOK: 1½ hours, plus standing time

85 g/3 oz wholemilk natural yogurt

1 tbsp each garlic paste and ginger paste

700 g/1 lb 9 oz skinless, boneless chicken thighs

1 tbsp white poppy seeds

2 tsp coriander seeds

½ mace blade

2 bay leaves, torn into small pieces

½ tsp black peppercorns

1 tsp cardamom seeds

2.5-cm/1-inch piece cinnamon stick

4 cloves

55 g/2 oz ghee

1 large onion, finely sliced

1½ tsp salt, or to taste

fried onions, to garnish

RICE

pinch of saffron threads, pounded

2 tbsp hot milk

1½ tsp salt

2 x 5-cm/2-inch cinnamon sticks

3 star anise

2 bay leaves, crumbled

4 cloves

4 green cardamom pods, bruised

450 g/1 lb basmati rice, washed

1 Put the yogurt and the garlic and ginger pastes in a bowl and beat together with a fork until thoroughly blended. Put the chicken in a non-metallic bowl, add the yogurt mixture and mix until well combined. Cover and leave to marinate in the refrigerator for 2 hours.

2 Grind the next eight ingredients (all the seeds and spices) to a fine powder in a spice grinder and set aside.

3 In a flameproof casserole large enough to hold the chicken and the rice together, melt the ghee over a medium heat, add the onion and cook, stirring frequently, for 8–10 minutes, until a medium brown colour.

4 Reduce the heat to low, add the ground seeds and spices and cook, stirring, for 2–3 minutes. Add the marinated chicken and salt and cook, stirring, for 2 minutes. Turn off the heat and keep the chicken covered.

5 Meanwhile, place the pounded saffron in a small bowl with the hot milk and leave to infuse for 20 minutes.

6 Preheat the oven to 180°C/350°F/ Gas Mark 4. Bring a large saucepan of water to the boil and add the salt and spices. Add the rice, return to the boil and boil steadily for 2 minutes. Drain the rice, reserving the whole spices, and pile on top of the chicken. Pour the saffron and milk mixture over the rice.

7 Soak a piece of greaseproof paper large enough to cover the top of the rice fully and squeeze out the excess water. Lay on top of the rice. Soak a clean tea towel, wring out and lay loosely on top of the greaseproof paper. Cover the casserole with a piece of aluminium foil. It is important to cover the rice in this way to contain all the steam inside the casserole, as the biryani cooks entirely in the vapour created inside the casserole. Put the lid on top and cook in the centre of the preheated oven for 1 hour.

8 Turn off the oven and leave the rice to stand inside for 30 minutes. Transfer the biryani to serving plates and garnish with the fried onions.

Murgh xacuti

GOAN SPICED CHICKEN

Pronounced 'shakutee', this classic, spicy chicken dish from the shores of Goa can be found in almost all the restaurants that dot the beaches and villages and towns. Made from a blend of coconut milk, red chillies and aromatic spices, it is best served with some steamed rice and mango chutney.

SERVES: 4　　　　**PREP:** 20 minutes　　　　**COOK:** 35–40 minutes

6 black peppercorns

3 cloves

2 tsp fennel seeds

4 dried red chillies

1 tsp cardamom seeds

2 tsp white poppy seeds

2 cinnamon sticks

2 tsp salt

1 tsp ground turmeric

1 tsp ground cumin

1 tsp ground coriander

4 tbsp vegetable or groundnut oil

1 onion, very finely chopped

3 garlic cloves, crushed

600 g/1 lb 5 oz skinless, boneless chicken thighs, cut into bite-sized pieces

400 ml/14 fl oz coconut milk

300 ml/10 fl oz cold water

1 tsp tamarind paste

1 Place a large, non-stick frying pan over a medium heat and add the peppercorns, cloves, fennel seeds, dried red chillies, cardamom seeds, white poppy seeds and cinnamon sticks. Dry-fry for 1–2 minutes, then remove from the heat and allow to cool.

2 Place the cooled whole spices into a spice grinder with the salt, turmeric, cumin and ground coriander. Process until ground to a fairly fine powder.

3 Heat the oil in a large saucepan, add the onion and garlic and cook over a medium heat for 2–3 minutes. Increase the heat to high, add the chicken and stir-fry for 5–6 minutes, or until sealed.

4 Tip in the spice mixture and stir-fry for 1–2 minutes, then add the coconut milk and water. Bring to the boil, then reduce the heat to low–medium and simmer gently for 15–20 minutes. Stir in the tamarind paste and cook for a further 2–3 minutes, or until the chicken is cooked through and tender. Serve immediately.

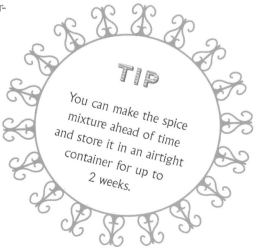

TIP

You can make the spice mixture ahead of time and store it in an airtight container for up to 2 weeks.

Rista

MEATBALLS IN CREAMY CASHEW NUT SAUCE

This delectable recipe comes from Kashmir, the most northerly state in India. This beautiful Himalayan state has a rich culinary heritage — Kashmiri cooking is a work of art and the chefs are extremely skilled as well as creative.

SERVES: 4

PREP: 25–30 minutes, plus soaking & chilling time

COOK: 35–40 minutes

125 g/4½ oz cashew nuts

150 ml/5 fl oz boiling water

450 g/1 lb fresh lean lamb mince

1 tbsp set natural yogurt

1 egg, beaten

½ tsp freshly ground cardamom seeds

½ tsp freshly ground nutmeg

½ tsp pepper

½ tsp dried mint

½ tsp salt, or to taste

300 ml/10 fl oz cold water

2.5-cm/1-inch piece cinnamon stick

5 green cardamom pods

5 cloves

2 bay leaves

3 tbsp vegetable or groundnut oil

1 onion, finely chopped

2 tsp garlic paste

1 tsp ground ginger

1 tsp ground fennel seeds

½ tsp ground turmeric

½–1 tsp chilli powder

150 ml/5 fl oz double cream

1 tbsp crushed pistachio nuts, to garnish

1 Soak the cashews in the boiling water for 20 minutes.

2 Put the lamb mince in a mixing bowl and add the yogurt, egg, ground cardamom seeds, nutmeg, pepper, mint and salt. Knead the mince until it is smooth and velvety. Alternatively, put the ingredients in a food processor and process until smooth and combined. Chill the mixture for 30–40 minutes, then divide it into quarters. Make five balls (koftas) out of each quarter, rolling them between your palms to make them smooth and firm.

3 Bring the cold water to the boil in a large, shallow pan and add all the whole spices and the bay leaves. Arrange the meatballs in a single layer in the spiced liquid. Reduce the heat to medium, cover the pan and cook for 12–15 minutes.

4 Remove the meatballs from the pan, cover and keep hot. Strain the spiced liquid and set aside.

5 Wipe out the pan and add the oil. Place over a medium heat and add the onion and garlic paste. Cook until the mixture begins to brown and add the ground ginger, ground fennel seeds, turmeric and chilli powder. Stir-fry for 2–3 minutes, then add the strained liquid and meatballs. Bring to the boil, reduce the heat to low, cover and simmer for 10–12 minutes.

6 Meanwhile, purée the cashews with their soaking water in a blender and add to the meatball mixture along with the cream. Simmer for a further 5–6 minutes, then remove from the heat. Garnish with the crushed pistachio nuts and serve immediately.

Keema mattar

SPICED LAMB MINCE WITH PEAS

When the cold winter winds come to northern India, this simple, rustic dish of minced lamb and peas cooked with warming spices makes a popular family meal. Serve with any Indian bread for a filling supper.

SERVES: 4–6

PREP: 5–10 minutes

COOK: 35–40 minutes

30 g/1 oz ghee or 2 tbsp vegetable or groundnut oil

2 tsp cumin seeds

1 large onion, finely chopped

½ tbsp garlic paste

½ tbsp ginger paste

2 bay leaves

1 tsp mild, medium or hot curry powder, to taste

2 tomatoes, deseeded and chopped

1 tsp ground coriander

¼–½ tsp chilli powder

¼ tsp ground turmeric

pinch of sugar

½ tsp salt

½ tsp pepper

500 g/1 lb 2 oz fresh lean lamb mince

250 g/9 oz frozen peas

1 Melt the ghee in a flameproof casserole or large frying pan with a tight-fitting lid. Add the cumin seeds and cook, stirring, for 30 seconds, or until they start to crackle.

2 Stir in the onion, garlic and ginger pastes, bay leaves and curry powder and continue to stir-fry until the fat separates.

3 Stir in the tomatoes and cook for 1–2 minutes. Add the ground coriander, chilli powder, turmeric, sugar, salt and pepper and stir around for 30 seconds.

4 Add the lamb mince and cook, using a wooden spoon to break up the meat, for 5 minutes, or until it is no longer pink. Reduce the heat and simmer, stirring occasionally, for 10 minutes.

5 Add the peas and simmer for a further 10–15 minutes, until the peas are heated through. If there is too much liquid left in the pan, increase the heat and let it bubble for a few minutes until it reduces.

Gosht dhansak

SWEET & SOUR LAMB WITH LENTILS

For India's numerous Parsis, this rich dish is served for a Sunday family lunch. The lentils and pumpkin dissolve into a velvety smooth sauce, and all that is needed to complete the meal are freshly cooked rice and naans.

SERVES: 4

PREP: 20–25 minutes, plus standing time

COOK: 45–50 minutes

700 g/1 lb 9 oz boneless lamb shoulder, trimmed and cut into 5-cm/2-inch cubes

2 tsp salt, or to taste

½ tbsp each garlic paste and ginger paste

5 green cardamom pods

200 g/7 oz yellow lentils (toor dal)

100 g/3½ oz pumpkin, peeled, deseeded and chopped

1 carrot, thinly sliced

1 fresh green chilli, deseeded and chopped

1 tsp fenugreek powder

500 ml/18 fl oz cold water, plus extra if needed

1 large onion, thinly sliced

30 g/1 oz ghee or 2 tbsp vegetable or groundnut oil

2 garlic cloves, crushed

chopped fresh coriander, to garnish

DHANSAK MASALA

1 tsp garam masala

½ tsp ground coriander

½ tsp ground cumin

½ tsp chilli powder

½ tsp ground turmeric

¼ tsp freshly ground cardamom seeds

¼ tsp ground cloves

1 Put the lamb and 1 teaspoon of the salt in a large saucepan with enough water to cover and bring to the boil. Reduce the heat and simmer, skimming the surface as necessary until no more foam rises. Stir in the garlic and ginger pastes and cardamom pods and continue simmering for a total of 30 minutes.

2 Meanwhile, put the lentils, pumpkin, carrot, chilli and fenugreek powder in a large, heavy-based saucepan and pour over the water. Bring to the boil, stirring occasionally, then reduce the heat and simmer for 20–30 minutes, until the lentils and carrot are very tender. Stir in a little extra water if the lentils look as though they will catch on the base of the pan. Leave the lentil mixture to cool slightly, then pour it into a food processor or blender and process until a thick, smooth sauce forms.

3 Put the onion in a bowl, sprinkle with the remaining teaspoon of salt and leave to stand for about 5 minutes. Use your hands to squeeze out the moisture from the onion.

4 Melt the ghee in a flameproof casserole or large frying pan with a tight-fitting lid over a high heat. Add the onion and cook, stirring constantly, for 2 minutes. Remove one third of the onion and continue frying the rest for a further 1–2 minutes, until golden brown. Use a slotted spoon to immediately remove the onion from the pan, as it will continue to darken as it cools. Set aside.

5 Return the one third of the onion to the pan with the garlic. Stir in all the dhansak masala ingredients and cook for 2 minutes, stirring constantly. Add the cooked lamb and stir for a further 2 minutes. Add the lentil sauce and simmer over a medium heat, stirring and adding a little extra water if needed, until warmed through. Taste and adjust the seasoning, adding extra salt if needed. Sprinkle with the reserved onion, garnish with chopped coriander and serve immediately.

Kashmiri gosht

KASHMIRI LAMB & FENNEL STEW

This slow-cooked, aromatic lamb stew from Kashmir in northern India almost cooks itself. Kashmiri chilli powder is available from Asian grocery stores, but you can make your own by finely grinding dried red Kashmiri chillies in a spice grinder.

SERVES: 4

PREP: 20 minutes

COOK: 2–2¼ hours

4 tbsp vegetable or groundnut oil

2 onions, halved and thinly sliced

600 g/1 lb 5 oz lamb shoulder, trimmed and cut into bite-sized pieces

4 garlic cloves, crushed

2 tsp finely grated fresh ginger

1 tbsp ground coriander

1 tsp Kashmiri chilli powder

1 tsp salt

300 g/10½ oz potatoes, halved

500 ml/18 fl oz lamb or chicken stock

200 ml/7 fl oz single cream

4 tbsp ground almonds

2 tbsp crushed fennel seeds

6 tbsp finely chopped fresh coriander

2 tbsp finely chopped fresh mint

1 Heat the oil in a non-stick saucepan and cook the onions over a low heat, stirring frequently, for about 15–20 minutes, until lightly browned.

2 Increase the heat to high, add the lamb and stir-fry for 4–5 minutes, until sealed. Reduce the heat to medium and add the garlic, ginger, ground coriander, chilli powder and salt. Stir and cook for 1–2 minutes.

3 Add the potatoes and stock, then cover and simmer over a low heat for about 1½ hours, or until the lamb is tender.

4 Uncover the pan, increase the heat slightly and stir in the cream and ground almonds. Cook for a further 8–10 minutes, until thickened and reduced. Take care not to boil or the cream will split.

5 Add the crushed fennel seeds to the pan and cook for a further 3–4 minutes. Remove from the heat and stir in the chopped coriander and mint. Serve immediately.

TIP

Use a heat diffuser under the pan for even heat distribution when slow-cooking – this prevents the dish from sticking to the base and getting burnt.

Kolhapuri gosht

KOLHAPURI MUTTON CURRY

This spicy curry originates from the town of Kolhapur in the western state of Maharashtra, which is known for its spicy fare. It is traditionally made with mutton, but you could use lamb if you prefer. Serve this tasty curry with freshly cooked basmati rice, a cooling cucumber raita and some tangy lime pickle.

SERVES: 4

PREP: 15–20 minutes, plus cooling time

COOK: 2 hours

3 tbsp vegetable or groundnut oil

600 g/1 lb 5 oz boneless mutton shoulder, trimmed and cut into bite-sized cubes

1 onion, thinly sliced

3 garlic cloves, crushed

1 tbsp finely grated fresh ginger

1 fresh red chilli, finely chopped

1 tsp ground turmeric

12 fresh curry leaves

400 g/14 oz canned chopped tomatoes

500 ml/18 fl oz lamb or chicken stock

100 ml/3½ fl oz coconut cream

3 tbsp finely chopped fresh coriander, plus extra to garnish

KOLHAPURI MASALA

2 tbsp coriander seeds

1 tbsp cumin seeds

1 tsp freshly ground cardamom seeds

4 cloves

2 cinnamon sticks

2 dried red chillies

¼ tsp freshly grated nutmeg

1 First, make the Kolhapuri masala. Place the coriander seeds, cumin seeds, cardamom seeds, cloves and cinnamon sticks in a non-stick frying pan over a low heat. Dry-fry the spices, shaking the pan, for 1 minute, or until fragrant. Remove from the heat and allow to cool, then place in a spice grinder with the dried red chilli and nutmeg. Grind to a powder and set aside.

2 Heat 1 tablespoon of the oil in a heavy-based saucepan over a medium–high heat. Brown the mutton, in batches, for 3–4 minutes. Remove the mutton from the pan with a slotted spoon and set aside.

3 Add the remaining oil to the pan and reduce the heat to medium. Cook the onion, stirring, for 2–3 minutes, until softened. Add the garlic, ginger, fresh red chilli, turmeric and curry leaves and cook for 1 minute, until fragrant.

4 Add the Kolhapuri masala and stir well to combine, then return the mutton to the pan, stirring to coat in the onion mixture. Add the chopped tomatoes and stock and bring to the boil. Reduce the heat to low and simmer, uncovered, for 1½ hours, or until the mutton is tender.

5 Stir in the coconut cream and chopped coriander, then cook for a further 10 minutes, or until the sauce has thickened. Garnish with extra chopped coriander and serve immediately.

TIP

Fresh curry leaves freeze well – simply place them in a freezer bag, seal and freeze. You can use them straight out of the freezer.

Vindaloo

PORK WITH CHILLIES, VINEGAR & GARLIC

The name *vindaloo* is derived from two Portuguese words — *vin*, meaning 'vinegar', and *alho*, meaning 'garlic'. When the Portuguese travelled to India, they took pork preserved in vinegar, garlic and pepper, which was spiced up to suit Indian tastes and this dish was born.

SERVES: 4

PREP: 15–20 minutes, plus marinating time

COOK: 1¼–1½ hours

2–6 dried red chillies, torn

5 cloves

2.5-cm/1-inch piece cinnamon stick, broken up

4 green cardamom pods

½ tsp black peppercorns

½ mace blade

¼ nutmeg, lightly crushed

1 tsp cumin seeds

1½ tsp coriander seeds

½ tsp fenugreek seeds

2 tsp garlic paste

1 tbsp ginger paste

3 tbsp cider vinegar or white wine vinegar

1 tbsp tamarind juice or juice of ½ lime

700 g/1 lb 9 oz boneless pork leg, cut into 2.5-cm/1-inch cubes

4 tbsp vegetable or groundnut oil, plus 2 tsp

2 large onions, finely chopped

300 ml/10 fl oz warm water

1 tsp salt, or to taste

1 tsp soft dark brown sugar

2 large garlic cloves, finely sliced

8–10 fresh curry leaves

1 Grind the first ten ingredients (all the spices) to a fine powder in a spice grinder. Transfer the ground spices to a bowl and add the garlic and ginger pastes, vinegar and tamarind juice. Mix together to form a paste.

2 Put the pork in a large, non-metallic bowl and rub about one quarter of the spice paste into the meat. Cover and leave to marinate in the refrigerator for 30–40 minutes.

3 Heat the 4 tablespoons of oil in a heavy-based saucepan over a medium heat, add the onions and cook, stirring frequently, for 8–10 minutes, until lightly browned. Add the remaining spice paste and cook, stirring constantly, for 5–6 minutes. Add 2 tablespoons of the water and cook until it evaporates. Repeat with another 2 tablespoons of water.

4 Add the marinated pork and cook over a medium–high heat for 5–6 minutes. Add the salt, sugar and the remaining water. Bring to the boil, then reduce the heat to low, cover and simmer for 50–55 minutes.

5 Meanwhile, heat the 2 teaspoons of oil in a small saucepan over a low heat. Add the sliced garlic and cook, stirring, until it begins to brown. Add the curry leaves and leave to sizzle for 15–20 seconds. Stir the garlic mixture into the pan. Serve immediately.

CHAPTER 4

PULSES

Rasam

SOUTH INDIAN LENTIL BROTH

Rice is a staple dish in south India and is served at almost every meal. It is usually accompanied by this spiced lentil broth and served with *pachadis* (south Indian raitas) and dry curried vegetables. *Rasam* is a very thin and liquid preparation that can also be eaten as a soup.

SERVES: 4

PREP: 10 minutes

COOK: 30–35 minutes

100 g / 3½ oz pigeon peas (tuvaar dal)
600 ml / 1 pint cold water
1 tsp ground turmeric
2 tbsp vegetable or groundnut oil
1 tsp black mustard seeds
6–8 fresh curry leaves
1 tsp cumin seeds
1 fresh green chilli
1 tsp tamarind paste
1 tsp salt

1 Rinse the pigeon peas under cold running water. Place the pigeon peas in a saucepan with the water, turmeric and 1 tablespoon of the oil. Cover and simmer for 25–30 minutes, or until the lentils are cooked and tender.

2 Heat the remaining oil in a frying pan over a medium heat. Add the mustard seeds, curry leaves, cumin seeds, chilli and tamarind paste. When the seeds start to pop, remove the pan from the heat and add to the lentil mixture with the salt.

3 Return the broth to the heat for 2–3 minutes. Ladle into small serving bowls and serve immediately with steamed basmati rice.

Tarka dal

LENTILS WITH CUMIN & SHALLOTS

This dish, traditionally known as *tarka dal,* is easy to cook. The word *tarka* means 'tempering' – the boiled dal is tempered with a few whole spices, and chopped shallots are added to the hot oil before being folded into the cooked lentils.

SERVES: 4

PREP: 10–15 minutes

COOK: 1 hour

200 g/7 oz split red lentils (masoor dal)

850 ml/1½ pints cold water

1 tsp salt, or to taste

2 tsp vegetable or groundnut oil

½ tsp black or brown mustard seeds

½ tsp cumin seeds

4 shallots, finely chopped

2 fresh green chillies, chopped (deseeded if you like)

1 tsp ground turmeric

1 tsp ground cumin

1 fresh tomato, chopped

2 tbsp chopped fresh coriander

1 Place the lentils in a sieve and rinse under cold running water. Drain and put into a saucepan. Add the water and bring to the boil. Reduce the heat to medium and skim the surface to remove the foam. Cook, uncovered, for 10 minutes. Reduce the heat to low, cover and cook, stirring occasionally to ensure that the lentils do not stick to the base of the pan as they thicken, for 45 minutes. Stir in the salt.

2 Meanwhile, heat the oil in a small saucepan over a medium heat. When hot, but not smoking, add the mustard seeds, followed by the cumin seeds. Add the shallots and chillies and cook, stirring, for 2–3 minutes, then add the turmeric and ground cumin. Add the tomato and cook, stirring, for 30 seconds.

3 Fold the shallot mixture into the cooked lentils. Stir in the chopped coriander, remove from the heat and serve immediately.

Moong dal khichdee

YELLOW SPLIT MUNG BEAN & RICE PILAFF

This classic Gujarati rice and lentil preparation is a warming and comforting dish, particularly when one is feeling low or ill. It is delicious served with a dollop of natural yogurt, green chilli pickle (see page 50) and your favourite chutney. Split yellow mung beans are widely available and do not require soaking.

SERVES: 4

200 g/7 oz split yellow mung beans (moong dal)

200 g/7 oz basmati rice

25 g/1 oz ghee or 2 tbsp vegetable or groundnut oil

6–8 black peppercorns

2 tsp cumin seeds

4 garlic cloves, finely chopped

2 tsp salt

¼ tsp ground turmeric

1 litre/1¾ pints boiling water

PREP: 10 minutes

1 Place the mung beans and rice in a sieve and rinse under cold running water. Drain and set aside.

2 Heat the ghee in a heavy-based saucepan over a medium heat. Add the reserved mung bean and rice mixture and stir-fry gently for 1–2 minutes.

3 Add the peppercorns, cumin seeds, garlic, salt and turmeric and stir-fry for 1–2 minutes. Pour in the water.

COOK: 20–25 minutes, plus standing time

4 Bring to the boil, then cover tightly and reduce the heat to low. Cook, without stirring, for 12–15 minutes, then remove from the heat (without lifting the lid) and allow to stand for 12–15 minutes.

5 To serve, remove the lid and gently fluff up the grains with a fork. Serve immediately.

TIP

For a variation on this recipe, you can replace the split yellow mung beans with split red lentils (masoor dal).

Ma ki dal

SPICED BLACK LENTILS

Using whole black lentils with their skins still on, rather than split lentils, adds a gelatinous texture to this rich dish. It is time-consuming so is more likely to be prepared for a special occasion than on an everyday basis.

SERVES: 4–6

PREP: 10–15 minutes, plus soaking time

COOK: 3½ hours

250 g / 9 oz whole black lentils (urad dal sabat)

115 g / 4 oz dried red kidney beans

4 garlic cloves, cut in half

4 black cardamom pods, lightly crushed

2 bay leaves

1 cinnamon stick

115 g / 4 oz butter

¾ tsp garlic paste

¾ tsp ginger paste

2 tbsp tomato purée

½ tsp chilli powder

pinch of sugar

150 ml / 5 fl oz double cream

salt

fresh coriander sprigs, to garnish

1 Put the lentils and kidney beans in separate bowls with plenty of water to cover and leave to soak for at least 3 hours, but preferably overnight.

2 Meanwhile, put the garlic cloves, cardamom pods, bay leaves and cinnamon stick in a piece of muslin and tie together into a bundle.

3 Drain the lentils and kidney beans separately. Put the kidney beans in a large saucepan with twice their volume of water and bring to the boil, then boil for 10 minutes. Drain well.

4 Return the kidney beans to the pan, add the black lentils and cover with double their volume of water. Add the spice bag and bring to the boil over a high heat. Reduce the heat to low, partially cover the pan and simmer, skimming the surface as necessary to remove the foam, for about 3 hours, until the pulses are very tender and reduced to a thick paste. Mash the pulses against the side of the pan with a wooden spoon every 15 minutes while they are simmering and stir in extra water if it evaporates before the pulses are tender.

5 When the pulses are almost cooked, remove the spice bag and set aside to cool.

6 Melt the butter in a small pan. Add the garlic and ginger pastes and stir around for 1 minute. Stir in the tomato purée, chilli powder, sugar and salt to taste and continue simmering for 2–3 minutes.

7 When the spice bag is cool enough to handle, squeeze all the flavouring juices into the pulses. Stir the butter and spice mixture into the pulses, along with all but 2 tablespoons of the cream. Bring to the boil, then reduce the heat and simmer, stirring occasionally, for 10 minutes.

8 Transfer the dal to a serving dish, then swirl over the remaining cream and garnish with coriander sprigs.

Khichdee
KITCHRI

This recipe makes a light meal on its own, served with Indian bread and a raita, but it is also excellent to team with other vegetarian dishes. This is the traditional Indian dish that British cooks of the Raj adapted into kedgeree.

SERVES: 4–6

225 g/8 oz basmati rice
250 g/9 oz split red lentils (masoor dal)
30 g/1 oz ghee or 2 tbsp vegetable or groundnut oil
1 large onion, finely chopped
2 tsp garam masala
1½ tsp salt, or to taste
pinch of asafoetida
850 ml/1½ pints cold water
2 tbsp chopped fresh coriander

PREP: 5–10 minutes, plus soaking time

1 Rinse the rice in several changes of water until the water runs clear, then leave to soak for 30 minutes. Drain and set aside until ready to cook.

2 Meanwhile, place the lentils in a sieve and rinse under cold running water. Drain and set aside.

3 Melt the ghee in a flameproof casserole or a large saucepan over a medium–high heat. Add the onion and stir-fry for 5–8 minutes, until golden but not brown.

4 Add the reserved rice and lentils along with the garam masala, salt and asafoetida, and stir for 2 minutes. Pour in the water and bring to the boil, stirring.

COOK: 35–40 minutes, plus standing time

5 Reduce the heat to the lowest setting and cover the pan tightly. Simmer, without lifting the lid, for 20 minutes, until the grains are tender and the liquid is absorbed. Re-cover the pan, turn off the heat and leave to stand for 5 minutes.

6 Use a fork to fluff up the grains of rice. Mix in the chopped coriander and adjust the seasoning, adding extra salt if needed. Serve immediately.

Cholar dal
SPICED BENGAL GRAM

Traditionally eaten during religious celebrations, this spiced dal from Bengal is delicious with pooris or rice. The lentils used in this preparation are commonly known as split yellow lentils or *chana dal* but they are sometimes referred to as Bengal gram. They do not need overnight soaking before cooking.

SERVES: 4

PREP: 15 minutes

COOK: 40–45 minutes

250 g/9 oz split yellow lentils (chana dal)

850 ml/1½ pints cold water, plus extra if needed

75 g/2¾ oz ghee

1 small onion, very finely diced

2 fresh green chillies, slit lengthways

1 tbsp ground coriander

1 tsp ground cumin

2 bay leaves

1 tsp hot chilli powder

1 tsp ground turmeric

2 dried red chillies

2 garlic cloves, very finely sliced

2 tsp grated fresh ginger

1 tbsp raisins

2 tsp salt

2 tbsp lightly toasted desiccated coconut, to garnish

1 Place the lentils in a sieve and rinse under cold running water. Drain.

2 Place the lentils and water in a saucepan, stir well and bring to the boil, skimming the surface as necessary to remove the foam. Reduce the heat, cover and simmer, stirring frequently and adding more water if needed, for 35–40 minutes, or until the lentils are just tender.

3 Remove the pan from the heat and use a whisk to break down the lentils. Set aside and keep warm.

4 Meanwhile, heat the ghee in a non-stick frying pan over a medium heat. Add the onion and stir-fry for 4–5 minutes.

5 Add the fresh green chillies, ground coriander, cumin, bay leaves, chilli powder, turmeric, dried red chillies, garlic and ginger and stir-fry for 1–2 minutes. Add the raisins, stir and cook for 30 seconds.

6 Remove from the heat and pour the spice mixture over the lentils. Stir in the salt, mix well and heat through. Garnish with the toasted coconut and serve immediately.

Khatti meethi dal

SWEET & SOUR LENTILS

Indian cooks never seem to run out of ideas for making something special out of simple, cheap ingredients. This is another Bengali style of preparing split yellow lentils with sweet flavours from the coconut and sugar, and sour flavours from the asafoetida and tamarind.

SERVES: 4

PREP: 5–10 minutes

COOK: 1 hour

250 g/9 oz split yellow lentils (chana dal)

1.2 litres/2 pints cold water

2 bay leaves, torn

3 fresh green chillies, slit lengthways

½ tsp ground turmeric

½ tsp asafoetida

3 tbsp vegetable or groundnut oil

½ onion, finely chopped

2-cm/¾-inch piece fresh ginger, finely chopped

30 g/1 oz creamed coconut, grated

1 fresh green chilli, chopped (deseeded if you like)

1½ tbsp sugar, or to taste

1½ tbsp tamarind paste, or to taste

½ tsp garam masala

¼ tsp ground cumin

¼ tsp ground coriander

salt

GARNISH

15 g/½ oz ghee, melted

1 tsp garam masala

2 tbsp chopped fresh coriander

1 Place the lentils in a sieve and rinse under cold running water. Drain and put into a large saucepan with the water. Place over a high heat and bring to the boil, skimming the surface as necessary to remove the foam. When the foam stops rising, stir in the bay leaves, whole green chillies, turmeric and asafoetida. Partially cover the pan and continue to simmer for about 40 minutes, or until the lentils are tender and the liquid has been absorbed.

2 Meanwhile, heat the oil in a large frying pan over a medium–high heat. Add the onion and ginger and stir-fry for 5–8 minutes. Stir in the creamed coconut, chopped green chilli, sugar, tamarind paste, garam masala, cumin and ground coriander and stir for about 1 minute.

3 Add the cooked lentils to the spice mixture and stir well to combine. Taste and adjust the seasoning, adding salt to taste and extra sugar and tamarind if needed.

4 Transfer the lentils to a serving dish and drizzle the melted ghee over the top. Sprinkle with the garam masala and chopped coriander and serve immediately.

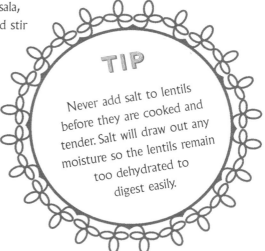

TIP

Never add salt to lentils before they are cooked and tender. Salt will draw out any moisture so the lentils remain too dehydrated to digest easily.

Masala dal

MIXED LENTILS WITH FIVE-SPICE SEASONING

Bengali five-spice seasoning, or *panch phoran*, is a typical combination of spices used in eastern and north-eastern India. Here the whole spices are fried briefly in hot oil to release their fragrant aromas and added to the cooked dal to 'temper' it.

SERVES: 4–6

PREP: 5–10 minutes

COOK: 30–35 minutes

125 g/4½ oz split red lentils (masoor dal)

125 g/4½ oz split yellow mung beans (moong dal)

850 ml/1½ pints hot water, plus extra if needed

1 tsp ground turmeric

1 tsp salt

1 tbsp lemon juice

2 tbsp vegetable or groundnut oil

¼ tsp black mustard seeds

¼ tsp cumin seeds

¼ tsp nigella seeds

¼ tsp fennel seeds

4–5 fenugreek seeds

2–3 dried red chillies

GARNISH

1 small tomato, deseeded and cut into strips

fresh coriander sprigs

1 Place the lentils and mung beans in a sieve and rinse under cold running water. Drain and put them into a saucepan with the water. Bring to the boil, then reduce the heat slightly and boil for 5–6 minutes, skimming the surface as necessary to remove the foam. When the foam stops rising, add the turmeric, reduce the heat to low, cover and cook for 20 minutes. Add the salt and lemon juice and beat the dal with a whisk. Add a little more water if the dal is too thick.

2 Heat the oil in a small saucepan over a medium heat. When hot, but not smoking, add the mustard seeds. As soon as they begin to pop, reduce the heat to low and add the cumin seeds, nigella seeds, fennel seeds, fenugreek seeds and dried chillies. Allow the spices to sizzle until the seeds begin to pop and the chillies have blackened. Remove from the heat immediately.

3 Transfer the cooked lentils to a serving dish. Pour over the spice mixture, scraping off every bit from the pan. Garnish with the tomato strips and coriander sprigs and serve immediately.

Vatana gashi

CHICKPEAS IN COCONUT MILK

This simple but delicious dish hails from the palm-fringed southern coast of India, where coconut milk is used as an everyday stock. Traditionally, dried chickpeas would be used, but canned ones are a time-saving alternative.

SERVES: 4

PREP: 5–10 minutes

COOK: 15–20 minutes

275 g / 9¾ oz potatoes, cut into 1-cm / ½-inch cubes

250 ml / 9 fl oz hot water

400 g / 14 oz canned chickpeas, drained and rinsed

250 ml / 9 fl oz coconut milk

1 tsp salt

2 tbsp vegetable or groundnut oil

4 large garlic cloves, finely chopped or crushed

2 tsp ground coriander

½ tsp ground turmeric

½–1 tsp chilli powder

juice of ½ lemon

1 Put the potatoes in a saucepan and pour over the water. Bring to the boil, then reduce the heat to low and cook, covered, for 6–7 minutes, until the potatoes are almost cooked through. Add the chickpeas and cook, uncovered, for 3–4 minutes, until the potatoes are tender. Add the coconut milk and salt and bring to a slow simmer.

2 Meanwhile, heat the oil in a small saucepan over a low heat. Add the garlic and cook, stirring frequently, until it begins to brown. Add the ground coriander, turmeric and chilli powder and cook, stirring, for 25–30 seconds.

3 Fold the spiced oil into the chickpea mixture. Stir in the lemon juice and remove from the heat. Serve immediately.

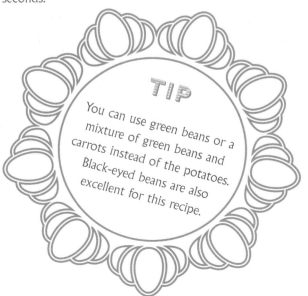

TIP

You can use green beans or a mixture of green beans and carrots instead of the potatoes. Black-eyed beans are also excellent for this recipe.

Chhole tamattar

CHICKPEAS WITH SPICED TOMATOES

In the Punjab, chickpeas are popular all year round and are often included in Sikh festive meals. Here they are made into a versatile salad that can be enjoyed as part of a vegetarian meal.

SERVES: 4

PREP: 10–15 minutes

COOK: 25–30 minutes

6 tbsp vegetable or groundnut oil

2 tsp cumin seeds

3 large onions, finely chopped

1 tsp garlic paste

1 tsp ginger paste

2 small fresh green chillies, deseeded and thinly sliced

1½ tsp dried mango powder (amchoor)

1½ tsp garam masala

¾ tsp asafoetida

½ tsp ground turmeric

¼–1 tsp chilli powder

3 large, firm tomatoes, about 450 g/1 lb, grated

800 g/1 lb 12 oz canned chickpeas, drained and rinsed

6 tbsp water

300 g/10½ oz fresh spinach leaves, tough stalks removed

½ tsp salt, or to taste

1 Heat the oil in a large frying pan over a medium–high heat. Add the cumin seeds and stir around for 30 seconds, or until they brown and crackle, watching carefully because they can burn quickly.

2 Add the onions, garlic and ginger pastes and chillies and stir-fry for 5–8 minutes, until the onions are golden.

3 Stir in the dried mango powder, garam masala, asafoetida, turmeric and chilli powder. Add the tomatoes to the pan and continue to cook, stirring frequently, until the sauce blends together and starts to brown slightly.

4 Stir in the chickpeas and water and bring to the boil. Reduce the heat to very low and use a wooden spoon or a potato masher to mash about a quarter of the chickpeas, leaving the remainder whole.

5 Add the spinach to the pan and stir until it begins to wilt. Stir in the salt, then taste and adjust the seasoning, adding extra salt if needed. Serve immediately.

TIP

Grating tomatoes is a simple way to eliminate tough pieces of tomato skin from a dish without having to peel them.

Chaat

CHICKPEAS WITH POTATO & SPICED YOGURT

This sweet, yet savoury, and slightly spicy dish can be found all over India. The base is a store-bought, crispy-fried puffed 'cracker' called *panipuri*, which is available from Asian grocery stores. If you cannot get hold of them, you can use any thin, wheat crackers you can find. *Sev* are thin, crispy strands of spiced, fried chickpea flour.

SERVES: 4

PREP: 20 minutes, plus soaking time

COOK: 25–30 minutes

200 g/7 oz dried chickpeas

400 g/14 oz wholemilk natural yogurt

1 tsp grated fresh ginger

1 tsp chilli powder

½ tsp ground cumin

½ tsp ground coriander

1 tsp salt

¼ tsp pepper

32 panipuris or thin, wheat crackers

2 large potatoes, peeled, boiled and roughly mashed

5 tbsp sweet chilli sauce

5 tbsp coriander chutney (see page 40)

1 small red onion, very finely diced

4 tbsp finely chopped fresh coriander

4 tbsp sev

2 tbsp pomegranate seeds

1 Soak the chickpeas in a bowl of cold water for 6–8 hours, or overnight. Drain, then place the chickpeas in a saucepan of cold water and bring to the boil. Cook for 25–30 minutes, or until tender. Drain well and set aside

2 Whisk the yogurt in a bowl until smooth, then stir in the ginger, chilli powder, ground cumin, ground coriander, salt and pepper. Set aside.

3 Break each panipuri gently with a fork to create a tiny opening on the top. Arrange the panipuris in a single layer on a large serving platter.

4 Place a spoonful of the potato on top of each panipuri. Divide the chickpeas between the panipuri and drizzle over the spiced yogurt. Spoon the sweet chilli sauce and coriander chutney on top. Scatter over the red onion, chopped coriander and sev. Finally, scatter over the pomegranate seeds and serve immediately.

TIP

You can prepare the chickpeas and spiced yogurt for this dish in advance but the rest must be assembled just before serving.

Rajma

RED KIDNEY BEAN CURRY

High in fibre, this delicious northern Indian dish of spiced red kidney beans is best served with rice and warmed flatbreads. It can easily be made a day ahead — simply prepare it up to the end of step 3. When you are ready to serve, simply warm it through and add the yogurt and chopped coriander.

SERVES: 4   **PREP:** 20 minutes   **COOK:** 30–35 minutes

2 tbsp vegetable or groundnut oil

2 tsp cumin seeds

2 onions, finely chopped

2 tsp grated fresh ginger

6 garlic cloves, crushed

2 fresh green chillies, finely chopped

2 large tomatoes, roughly chopped

2 tsp ground coriander

1 tsp ground cumin

¼ tsp ground turmeric

1 tsp garam masala

800 g/1 lb 12 oz canned red kidney beans, drained and rinsed

1 tsp palm sugar

500 ml/18 fl oz warm water

1 tsp salt

4 tbsp finely chopped fresh coriander, to garnish

natural yogurt, to serve

1 Heat the oil in a large saucepan and add the cumin seeds. When they stop crackling, add the onions and fry until they are soft.

2 Add the ginger and garlic and fry for 2 minutes. Add the green chillies, tomatoes, ground coriander, cumin, turmeric and garam masala and stir-fry for 12–15 minutes.

3 Add the red kidney beans, palm sugar, water and salt and cook for 10–12 minutes, or until the beans are soft.

4 Remove from the heat and transfer to a serving dish. Garnish with the chopped coriander and serve with a dollop of yogurt.

TIP

Canned beans are used in this recipe for speed. If using dried beans, cook according to the packet instructions before using.

CHAPTER 5
RICE & BREADS

Pulao

PILAU RICE

Colourful pilau rice is the perfect accompaniment to a whole range of Indian dishes. For the authentic flavour and texture it is important to use basmati rice, rather than any other long-grain rice. Don't be tempted to skip the soaking stage.

SERVES: 2–4

200 g/7 oz basmati rice
30 g/1 oz ghee
3 green cardamom pods
2 cloves
3 black peppercorns
½ tsp salt
½ tsp saffron threads
400 ml/14 fl oz cold water

PREP: 5 minutes, plus soaking time

1 Wash the rice in several changes of water until the water runs clear, then leave to soak in a bowl of fresh cold water for 30 minutes. Drain and set aside.

2 Melt the ghee in a heavy-based saucepan over a medium–high heat. Add the cardamom pods, cloves and peppercorns and stir-fry for 1 minute. Add the rice and stir-fry for a further 2 minutes.

COOK: 25–30 minutes

3 Add the salt, saffron and water to the rice mixture. Bring to the boil, then reduce the heat to low, cover and simmer for 20 minutes, until all the water has been absorbed.

4 Use a fork to fluff up the grains of rice. Transfer to a large serving dish and serve hot.

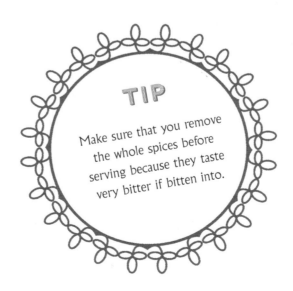

TIP

Make sure that you remove the whole spices before serving because they taste very bitter if bitten into.

Dahi bhaat

SPICED RICE WITH YOGURT & CUCUMBER

This delightful dish from southern India consists of rice combined with a seasoned yogurt and cucumber mixture and finished off with a tempered spiced oil (also known as *tarka*). Serve on its own or with curried vegetables and a fresh relish.

SERVES: 4

PREP: 25 minutes

COOK: 15 minutes, plus standing time

300 g/10½ oz basmati rice

55 g/2 oz ghee

2 tsp salt

600 ml/1 pint boiling water

2 fresh green chillies, split lengthways and deseeded

1 tbsp finely chopped fresh ginger

4 tbsp cold water

400 ml/14 fl oz set natural yogurt, whisked

6 tbsp finely chopped fresh coriander

1 tsp sugar

½ cucumber, finely diced

1 tsp white lentils (urad dal) (optional)

2 tsp black mustard seeds

2 tsp cumin seeds

2 dried red chillies

6–8 fresh curry leaves

2 garlic cloves, very thinly sliced

1 Place the rice in a heavy-based saucepan with 15 g/½ oz of the ghee and 1 teaspoon of the salt and pour over the boiling water. Bring to the boil, then reduce the heat to very low, cover tightly and simmer for 10–12 minutes. Remove from the heat and allow to stand, without lifting the lid, for 12–15 minutes.

2 Meanwhile, in a spice grinder or small food processor, blend together the chillies and ginger with the cold water until smooth.

3 Place the yogurt in a large bowl and add the chilli mixture along with the chopped coriander, sugar, cucumber and the remaining salt. Mix well.

4 When the rice has finished standing, uncover and fluff up the grains with a fork. Transfer to a serving dish, spoon over the yogurt mixture and toss to mix well.

5 Melt the remaining ghee in a frying pan. When hot, add the white lentils, if using, and the mustard seeds and cumin seeds. As soon as they start to pop, add the dried red chillies, curry leaves and garlic. Stir-fry for 30–40 seconds, then remove from the heat and pour the spiced oil over the rice mixture. Toss to mix well. Serve warm.

TIP

Leftover cooked rice is perfect to use in this recipe – warm it through until piping hot before using.

Nimbu chawal

LEMON-LACED BASMATI RICE

In this appetizing rice dish, the grains of basmati rice are tinged with yellow turmeric and adorned with black mustard seeds. The main flavour here is that of curry leaves, which is the hallmark of south Indian cuisine.

SERVES: 4

PREP: 5 minutes, plus soaking time

COOK: 12 minutes, plus standing time

225 g/8 oz basmati rice

2 tbsp vegetable or groundnut oil

½ tsp black or brown mustard seeds

10–12 fresh curry leaves

25 g/1 oz cashew nuts

¼ tsp ground turmeric

1 tsp salt

450 ml/16 fl oz hot water

2 tbsp lemon juice

1 tbsp snipped fresh chives, to garnish

1 Wash the rice in several changes of water until the water runs clear, then leave to soak in a bowl of fresh cold water for 20 minutes. Drain and set aside.

2 Heat the oil in a non-stick saucepan over a medium heat. When hot, but not smoking, add the mustard seeds, followed by the curry leaves and the cashew nuts (in that order).

3 Stir in the turmeric, quickly followed by the reserved rice and the salt. Cook, stirring, for 1 minute, then add the hot water and lemon juice. Stir once, bring to the boil and boil for 2 minutes.

4 Cover tightly, reduce the heat to very low and cook for 8 minutes. Turn off the heat and leave to stand, without lifting the lid, for 6–7 minutes.

5 Use a fork to fluff up the grains of rice. Transfer to a serving dish, garnish with the chives and serve immediately.

Chaunke hue chawal

SPICED BASMATI RICE

This delicately flavoured dish comes from Rajasthan in north-west India. It is particularly good served with lamb dishes. It is a good idea to remove the whole spices before serving because they taste bitter if bitten into.

SERVES: 4–6

PREP: 5 minutes, plus soaking time

COOK: 10–12 minutes, plus standing time

225 g/8 oz basmati rice

30 g/1 oz ghee or 2 tbsp vegetable or groundnut oil

5 green cardamom pods, bruised

5 cloves

½ cinnamon stick

1 tsp fennel seeds

½ tsp black mustard seeds

2 bay leaves

450 ml/16 fl oz cold water

1½ tsp salt, or to taste

pepper

1 Wash the rice in several changes of water until the water runs clear, then leave to soak in a bowl of fresh cold water for 30 minutes. Drain and set aside.

2 Melt the ghee in a large saucepan over a medium–high heat. Add the spices and bay leaves and stir for 30 seconds. Stir the reserved rice into the pan so the grains are coated with ghee.

3 Stir in the water and salt and bring to the boil. Reduce the heat to the lowest setting and cover the pan tightly. Simmer, without lifting the lid, for 8–10 minutes, until the grains are tender and all the liquid is absorbed.

4 Turn off the heat and use a fork to fluff up the grains of rice. Adjust the seasoning, adding extra salt and pepper to taste if needed. Re-cover the pan and leave to stand for 5 minutes before serving.

TIP

For spiced saffron rice, bring the water to the boil and stir in 1 teaspoon of saffron threads. Leave to infuse while the rice soaks, then add to the pan in step 3.

Vangi bhaat

AUBERGINE & TOMATO RICE

This one-pot rice dish from Maharashtra makes a delicious accompaniment to curries, but is even good when eaten on its own with a big dollop of yogurt and a crisp poppadom. Variations of this dish can be found throughout southern India, especially in the states of Andhra Pradesh and Karnataka.

SERVES: 4

275 g / 9¾ oz basmati rice

4 tbsp vegetable or groundnut oil

25 g / 1 oz ghee

4 shallots, finely chopped

2 garlic cloves, finely chopped

1 cinnamon stick

4 green cardamom pods

3 cloves

2 tsp cumin seeds

1 aubergine, trimmed and cut into 1-cm / ½-inch dice

4 ripe tomatoes, skinned, deseeded and finely chopped

2 tsp salt

1 tsp pepper

600 ml / 1 pint boiling water

6 tbsp finely chopped fresh coriander

PREP: 25 minutes, plus soaking time

1. Wash the rice in several changes of water until the water runs clear, then leave to soak in a bowl of fresh cold water for 20 minutes. Drain and set aside.

2. Heat the oil and ghee in a heavy-based saucepan over a medium heat. Fry the shallots, garlic, cinnamon stick, cardamom pods, cloves and cumin seeds for 4–5 minutes, until soft and fragrant.

3. Add the aubergine and stir-fry over a medium heat for 4–5 minutes. Add the tomatoes and the reserved rice and stir to mix well. Add the salt and pepper and pour over the water. Bring to the boil, then cover the pan tightly, reduce the heat to low and cook for 10–12 minutes. Remove from the heat and leave to stand, without lifting the lid, for 10 minutes.

COOK: 20–25 minutes, plus standing time

4. When ready to serve, uncover and use a fork to fluff up the grains of rice. Stir in the chopped coriander and serve immediately.

Thengai sadam

COCONUT RICE

Thanks to the abundance of coconut palms in the southern coastal regions of India, coconut — in its various guises — is a common ingredient in southern Indian cuisine. However, it also plays an essential role in religious ceremonies throughout India and South Asia. Fittingly, this dish is ideal for special occasions.

SERVES: 4–6

225 g/8 oz basmati rice
450 ml/16 fl oz water
60 g/2¼ oz creamed coconut
2 tbsp mustard oil
1½ tsp salt, or to taste

PREP: 5–10 minutes, plus soaking time

1 Wash the rice in several changes of water until the water runs clear, then leave to soak in a bowl of fresh cold water for 30 minutes. Drain and set aside.

2 Bring the water to the boil in a small saucepan, stir in the creamed coconut until it dissolves and set aside.

3 Heat the mustard oil in a large saucepan over a high heat until it smokes. Turn off the heat and leave the mustard oil to cool completely.

4 When you are ready to cook, reheat the mustard oil over a medium–high heat. Add the reserved rice and stir until the grains are coated in oil. Add the dissolved coconut and bring to the boil.

COOK: 15–20 minutes, plus standing time

5 Reduce the heat to its lowest setting, stir in the salt and cover the pan tightly. Simmer, without lifting the lid, for 8–10 minutes, until the rice is tender and all the liquid has been absorbed.

6 Turn off the heat and use a fork to fluff up the grains of rice. Taste and adjust the seasoning, adding extra salt if needed. Re-cover the pan and leave the rice to stand for 5 minutes before serving.

Mirch-dhaniye ke naan

CHILLI-CORIANDER NAAN

Naan is a type of leavened flatbread that came to India with the ancient Persians — it means 'bread' in their language. Naan is traditionally made by slapping the rolled and shaped dough against the hot inside of a charcoal-heated tandoor oven, but it can also be cooked under a very hot grill.

MAKES: 8

PREP: 20–25 minutes, plus resting time

COOK: 30–35 minutes

450 g/1 lb plain flour

2 tsp sugar

1 tsp salt

1 tsp baking powder

1 egg

250 ml/9 fl oz milk

2 tbsp vegetable or groundnut oil, plus extra for brushing

2 fresh red chillies, chopped (deseeded if you like)

15 g/½ oz fresh coriander leaves, chopped

25 g/1 oz ghee or butter, melted

1 Sift the flour, sugar, salt and baking powder into a large bowl. Whisk the egg and milk together, then gradually add to the flour mixture and stir until a dough is formed.

2 Transfer the dough to a work surface, make a depression in the centre of the dough and add the oil. Knead for 3–4 minutes, until you have a smooth and pliable dough. Wrap the dough in clingfilm and leave to rest for 1 hour.

3 Divide the dough into eight equal-sized pieces, form each piece into a ball and flatten into a thick cake. Cover with clingfilm and leave to rest for 10–15 minutes.

4 Preheat the grill to high, line a grill pan with aluminium foil and brush with oil. Roll each flattened cake into a 12.5-cm/5-inch round and pull the lower end gently. Carefully roll out again, maintaining the teardrop shape, until about 23 cm/9 inches long.

5 Mix the chillies and coriander together, then spread over the surface of the naans. Press gently so that the mixture sticks to the dough. Transfer a naan to the prepared grill pan and cook until slightly puffed and brown. Turn over and cook the other side, until lightly browned. Remove from the grill and brush with the melted ghee. Wrap in a tea towel while you cook the remaining naans.

Chapattis

CHAPATTIS

In Indian homes, chapattis are made fresh every day, using a special flour known as *atta*. Asian grocery stores sell atta, but you can replace it with two-thirds wholemeal bread flour combined with one-third plain flour.

MAKES: 16

PREP: 20 minutes, plus resting time

COOK: 25–30 minutes

400 g/14 oz chapatti flour (atta), plus extra for dusting

1 tsp salt

½ tsp sugar

2 tbsp vegetable or groundnut oil

250 ml/9 fl oz lukewarm water

1 Mix the chapatti flour, salt and sugar together in a large bowl. Add the oil and work well into the flour mixture with your fingertips. Gradually add the water, mixing at the same time. When a dough is formed, transfer it to a work surface and knead for 4–5 minutes, or until all the excess moisture has been absorbed by the flour. Wrap the dough in clingfilm and leave to rest for 30 minutes.

2 Divide the dough in half, then cut each half into eight equal-sized pieces. Form each piece into a ball and flatten into a round cake. Dust each cake lightly with flour and roll out to a 15-cm/6-inch round. Keep the remaining cakes covered while you are working on one. The chapattis will cook better when freshly rolled out, so roll out and cook one at a time.

3 Preheat a heavy-based, cast-iron griddle or a large, heavy-based frying pan over a medium–high heat. Put a chapatti on the griddle and cook for 30 seconds. Using a fish slice, turn over and cook until bubbles begin to appear on the surface. Turn over again. Press the edges down gently with a clean cloth to encourage the chapatti to puff up — they will not always puff up, but this doesn't matter. Cook until brown patches appear on the underside. Remove from the griddle and keep hot by wrapping in a piece of aluminium foil lined with kitchen paper. Repeat until all the chapattis have been cooked.

Poori

POORIS

These deep-fried breads puff up to look like balloons when they go into the hot oil. Children love watching them being cooked, but do keep them at a safe distance. Pooris are perfect for serving with most Indian dishes.

MAKES: 12

PREP: 20–25 minutes, plus resting time

COOK: 20–25 minutes

225 g/8 oz wholemeal flour, sifted, plus extra for dusting

½ tsp salt

30 g/1 oz ghee or butter, melted

100–150 ml/3½–5 fl oz cold water

vegetable or groundnut oil, for deep-frying

1 Put the flour and salt into a bowl and drizzle the ghee over the surface. Gradually stir in the water until a stiff dough forms. Turn out the dough onto a lightly floured surface and knead for 10 minutes, or until it is smooth and elastic. Shape the dough into a ball and place it in a clean bowl, then cover with a damp tea towel and leave to rest for 20 minutes.

2 Divide the dough into 12 equal-sized pieces and roll each into a ball. Flatten each ball of dough between your palms, then thinly roll it out on a lightly floured surface into a 13-cm/5-inch round. Continue until all the dough balls have been rolled out.

3 Heat enough oil for deep-frying in a large saucepan or deep-fryer to 180–190°C/350–375°F, or until a cube of bread browns in 30 seconds. Drop a poori into the hot oil and fry for about 10 seconds, or until it puffs up. Use two large spoons to flip the poori over and spoon some hot oil over the top.

4 Use the spoons to lift the poori from the oil and let any excess oil drip back into the pan. Drain the poori on kitchen paper and serve immediately. Continue cooking until all the pooris have been fried, making sure the oil returns to the correct temperature before you add the next poori.

Besan ki roti

SPICED GRAM FLOUR FLATBREADS

These tasty flatbreads are prepared using equal quantities of gram flour, which is made from ground chickpeas, and wholemeal flour. They are nutritious, high in protein and delicious served warm with any vegetable, lentil or chicken curry.

MAKES: 8

PREP: 20 minutes, plus resting time

COOK: 25–30 minutes

115 g/4 oz wholemeal flour

115 g/4 oz gram flour, plus extra for dusting

2 tsp salt

2 tbsp finely chopped fresh coriander

2 fresh red chillies, finely chopped

2 tsp cumin seeds

1 tsp crushed coriander seeds

1 tsp ground turmeric

75 g/2¾ oz ghee or butter, melted, plus extra for brushing

200 ml/7 fl oz cold water

1 Sift the flours and salt into a large mixing bowl, adding the bran left in the bottom of the sieve. Add all the remaining ingredients, except the water. Mix together and gradually add the water to form a soft, pliable dough. Knead on a lightly floured surface for 1–2 minutes, then allow to rest for 10 minutes.

2 Divide the mixture into eight equal-sized balls, then roll out each into a 12–15-cm/4½–6-inch round. Brush the top of each with a little extra melted ghee.

3 Heat a non-stick, cast-iron griddle or heavy-based frying pan over a medium heat. When hot, cook the dough rounds, one at a time, for 1–2 minutes on each side, pressing down with a spatula. Remove from the griddle, transfer to a plate and cover with aluminium foil to keep warm while you cook the remaining flatbreads. Serve warm.

TIP

For a less spicy version of these flatbreads, simply omit the chilli from this recipe.

Parathas

PARATHAS

Parathas are shallow-fried, unleavened breads that are often prepared for special occasions and religious festivals. Made with lots of melted ghee, parathas have a flaky texture and are too rich for everyday meals — unless you don't worry about your waistline! For an Indian-style breakfast, try them with a bowl of yogurt.

MAKES: 8

PREP: 30 minutes, plus resting time

COOK: 25–30 minutes

225 g/8 oz wholemeal flour, sifted, plus extra for dusting

½ tsp salt

150–200 ml/5–7 fl oz cold water

140 g/5 oz ghee or butter, melted

1 Mix the flour and salt together in a large bowl and make a well in the centre. Gradually stir in enough of the water to make a stiff dough. Turn out the dough onto a lightly floured surface and knead for 10 minutes, or until smooth and elastic. Shape the dough into a ball and place in a large bowl, then cover with a damp tea towel and leave to rest for 20 minutes.

2 Divide the dough into eight equal-sized pieces. Lightly flour your hands and roll each piece of dough into a ball. Working with one ball of dough at a time, roll it out on a lightly floured surface to form a 13-cm/5-inch round. Brush the top of the dough with about 1½ teaspoons of the melted ghee. Fold the round in half to make a half-moon shape and brush the top again with melted ghee. Fold the half-moon shape in half again to make a triangle. Press the layers together.

3 Roll out the triangle on a lightly floured surface into a larger triangle that is about 18 cm/7 inches on each side. Flip the dough back and forth between your hands a couple of times, then cover with a damp tea towel and continue until all the dough is shaped and rolled.

4 Meanwhile, heat a large, dry frying pan or griddle over a high heat until very hot and a splash of water 'dances' when it hits the surface. Place a paratha in the pan and cook until bubbles appear on the surface. Flip the paratha over and brush the surface with melted ghee. Continue cooking until the bottom is golden brown, then flip the paratha over again and smear with more melted ghee. Use a fish slice to press down on the surface of the paratha so it cooks evenly.

5 Brush with more melted ghee and serve immediately, then repeat with the remaining parathas. Parathas are best served as soon as they come out of the pan, but they can be kept warm wrapped in aluminium foil for about 20 minutes.

Aloo gobhi parathas

PARATHAS STUFFED WITH POTATO & CAULIFLOWER

These tasty flatbreads are stuffed with a spiced potato and cauliflower mixture before being rolled again and cooked in the usual way. They are delicious eaten with a bowl of yogurt or a raita and pickle, and can be served as an accompaniment to any main dish.

MAKES: 8

PREP: 30 minutes, plus resting time

COOK: 35–40 minutes

225 g/8 oz wholemeal flour

100 g/3½ oz plain flour, plus extra for dusting

1 tsp freshly ground cardamom seeds

2 tsp salt

250 ml/9 fl oz warm buttermilk

150 g/5½ oz ghee or butter, melted

FILLING

2 tbsp vegetable or groundnut oil

2 tsp cumin seeds

1 tbsp hot curry powder

4 garlic cloves, crushed

2 tsp finely grated fresh ginger

150 g/5½ oz cauliflower florets, very finely chopped

2 tsp salt

2 potatoes, boiled, peeled and roughly mashed

6 tbsp finely chopped fresh coriander

1 First, make the filling. Heat the oil in a large frying pan over a medium heat. Add the cumin seeds, curry powder, garlic, ginger and cauliflower and stir-fry for 8–10 minutes, or until the cauliflower has softened. Add the salt and the mashed potatoes and stir well to mix evenly. Remove from the heat and stir in the chopped coriander. Leave to cool.

2 Sift together the flours, ground cardamom seeds and salt into a large bowl, adding the bran left in the bottom of the sieve. Make a well in the centre and pour in the buttermilk and 2 tablespoons of the melted ghee. Work into the flour mixture to make a soft dough. Knead on a lightly floured surface for 10 minutes and form into a ball. Put the dough into a large bowl, cover with a damp cloth and leave to rest for 20 minutes. Divide the dough into eight equal-sized balls, then roll out each into a 15-cm/6-inch round.

3 Place a little of the filling into the centre of each dough round and fold up the edges into the centre to enclose the filling. Press down lightly and, using a lightly floured rolling pin, roll out to make a 15-cm/6-inch paratha. Repeat with the remaining dough and filling.

4 Heat a non-stick, flat, cast-iron griddle or heavy-based frying pan over a medium heat. Brush each paratha with a little of the remaining melted ghee. Brush the griddle with a little melted ghee. Put a paratha in the griddle and cook for 1–2 minutes, pressing down with a spatula. Turn over, brush with a little more ghee and cook for a further 1–2 minutes, or until flecked with light brown spots. Remove from the griddle, transfer to a plate and cover with aluminium foil to keep warm while you cook the remaining parathas. Serve warm.

CHAPTER 6
DESSERTS & DRINKS

Aam ki kulfi

MANGO KULFI

Kulfi is a dairy-based dessert flavoured with fruits and nuts, in this case mangoes and pistachio nuts. Traditionally, it is made by reducing a large volume of milk to the consistency of condensed milk. This recipe is less labour-intensive, using evaporated milk and cream.

SERVES: 6

PREP: 5–10 minutes, plus cooling & chilling time

COOK: 10–15 minutes

375 g/13 oz evaporated milk

300 ml/10 fl oz single cream

25 g/1 oz ground almonds

115–140 g/4–5 oz sugar, to taste

450 g/1 lb mango purée

1 tsp freshly ground cardamom seeds

25 g/1 oz shelled unsalted pistachio nuts, to decorate

1 Pour the evaporated milk and cream into a heavy-based saucepan and stir to mix. Place over a medium heat. Mix the ground almonds and sugar together, then add to the evaporated milk mixture. Cook, stirring, for 6–8 minutes, until the mixture thickens slightly.

2 Remove from the heat and leave the mixture to cool completely, stirring from time to time to prevent a skin from forming. When completely cold, stir in the mango purée and ground cardamom.

3 Meanwhile, preheat a small saucepan over a medium heat, add the pistachio nuts and toast for 2–3 minutes. Leave to cool, then lightly crush. Store in an airtight container until required.

4 Fill six kulfi moulds with the mango mixture and freeze for 5–6 hours. Before serving, transfer to the refrigerator for 40 minutes, then invert onto serving plates. Serve sprinkled with the crushed pistachio nuts to decorate.

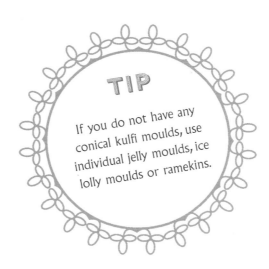

TIP

If you do not have any conical kulfi moulds, use individual jelly moulds, ice lolly moulds or ramekins.

Gajar ka halwa

SOFT CARROT FUDGE

This delicious dessert is made by cooking grated carrots in thickened milk to a soft, fudge-like consistency. A variety of contrasts in taste and texture is created by adding raisins, mixed nuts, cardamom, nutmeg and rosewater.

SERVES: 4–6

PREP: 15 minutes, plus cooling time

COOK: 20–25 minutes

55 g/2 oz ghee or unsalted butter

2.5-cm/1-inch piece cinnamon stick, halved

25 g/1 oz flaked almonds

25 g/1 oz cashew nuts

25 g/1 oz raisins

450 g/1 lb grated carrots

600 ml/1 pint full-fat milk

125 g/4½ oz caster sugar

½ tsp freshly ground cardamom seeds

½ tsp freshly grated nutmeg

50 ml/2 fl oz double cream

2 tbsp rosewater

vanilla ice cream or whipped cream, to serve

1 Melt the ghee in a heavy-based saucepan over a low heat. Add the cinnamon stick and leave to sizzle gently for 25–30 seconds. Add the flaked almonds and cashew nuts and cook, stirring, until lightly browned. Remove about a dessertspoon of the nuts and set aside.

2 Add the raisins, carrots, milk and sugar to the saucepan, increase the heat to medium and bring the milk to boiling point. Continue to cook over a low–medium heat for 15–20 minutes, until the milk evaporates completely, stirring frequently and blending in any thickened milk that sticks to the side of the saucepan. Don't allow any milk that is stuck to the side to brown or burn, as this will give the dessert an unpleasant flavour.

3 Stir in the ground cardamom, nutmeg, cream and rosewater. Remove from the heat and leave to cool slightly, then serve immediately topped with a scoop of ice cream or a dollop of whipped cream. Sprinkle the reserved nuts on top to decorate.

Firni

INDIAN RICE DESSERT

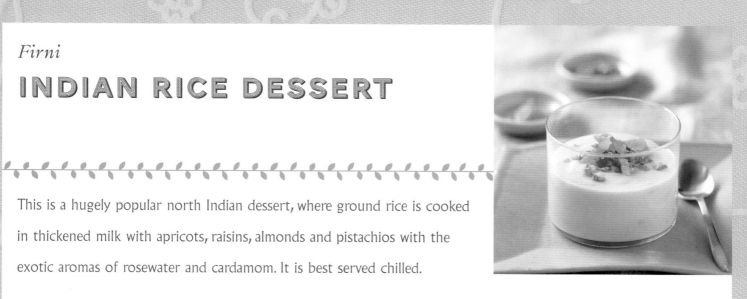

This is a hugely popular north Indian dessert, where ground rice is cooked in thickened milk with apricots, raisins, almonds and pistachios with the exotic aromas of rosewater and cardamom. It is best served chilled.

SERVES: 4

PREP: 10–15 minutes, plus cooling & chilling time

COOK: 20–25 minutes

good pinch of saffron threads, pounded

2 tbsp hot milk

40 g/1½ oz ghee or unsalted butter

55 g/2 oz ground rice

25 g/1 oz flaked almonds

25 g/1 oz raisins

600 ml/1 pint full-fat milk

450 g/1 lb evaporated milk

55 g/2 oz caster sugar

12 ready-to-eat dried apricots, sliced

1 tsp freshly ground cardamom seeds

½ tsp freshly grated nutmeg

2 tbsp rosewater

TO DECORATE

25 g/1 oz walnut pieces

15 g/½ oz shelled unsalted pistachio nuts

1 Place the pounded saffron in the hot milk and leave to soak until needed. Reserve 2 teaspoons of the ghee and melt the remainder in a heavy-based saucepan over a low heat. Add the ground rice, flaked almonds and raisins and cook, stirring, for 2 minutes. Add the milk, increase the heat to medium and cook, stirring, until it begins to bubble gently. Reduce the heat to low and cook for 10–12 minutes, stirring frequently to prevent the mixture from sticking to the pan.

2 Add the evaporated milk, sugar and apricots, reserving a few slices to decorate. Cook, stirring, until the mixture thickens to the consistency of a pouring custard.

3 Add the reserved saffron and milk mixture, the ground cardamom, nutmeg and rosewater, stir to distribute well and remove from the heat. Leave to cool, then cover and chill in the refrigerator for at least 2 hours.

4 Melt the reserved ghee in a small saucepan over a low heat. Add the walnut pieces and cook, stirring, until they brown a little. Remove and drain on kitchen paper. Brown the pistachio nuts in the saucepan, remove and drain on kitchen paper. Leave the pistachio nuts to cool, then lightly crush.

5 Serve the dessert decorated with the fried nuts and the reserved apricot slices.

Dudh pak

CREAMY ALMOND, PISTACHIO & RICE PUDDING

There are many different versions of this creamy milk and rice pudding, which is originally from Gujarat. This version is scented with cardamom and flavoured with pistachios and almonds. It needs constant stirring, but is well worth the effort.

SERVES: 4

PREP: 5 minutes, plus resting time

COOK: 25–30 minutes, plus standing time

2 litres / 3½ pints full-fat milk
85 g / 3 oz basmati rice
100 g / 3½ oz golden caster sugar
1 tsp freshly ground cardamom seeds
6 tbsp finely chopped pistachio nuts
6 tbsp finely chopped blanched almonds

1 Pour the milk into a large, heavy-based saucepan and bring to the boil.

2 Add the rice and cook over a medium heat, stirring constantly, for 18–20 minutes, or until the rice is tender.

3 Add the sugar, stir and cook for a further 3–4 minutes.

4 Remove from the heat and stir in the ground cardamom and the nuts. Cover and leave to stand for 20 minutes before serving.

TIP

This dessert is usually eaten warm but it is equally delicious served chilled.

Malai khumani

MIXED NUT & DRIED FRUIT DESSERT POTS

This sweet and creamy dessert originates from the royal state of Hyderabad in south India. The decoration of edible silver or gold leaf (*varak*) is optional but it transforms this simple dessert into one worthy of any celebration, whether it is a wedding, birthday or religious festival.

SERVES: 4

PREP: 20 minutes, plus soaking & chilling time

COOK: 0 minutes

200 g/7 oz ready-to-eat dried apricots

100 g/3½ oz sultanas

100 ml/3½ fl oz orange juice

300 ml/10 fl oz double cream

4 tbsp golden caster sugar

1 tsp rosewater

4 tbsp finely chopped pistachio nuts

4 tbsp finely chopped walnuts

4 tbsp finely chopped hazelnuts

edible silver or gold leaf, to decorate (optional)

1 Roughly chop the apricots and place in a bowl with the sultanas and orange juice. Cover and leave to soak for 20 minutes.

2 In a separate bowl, whisk the cream, sugar and rosewater until the cream holds soft peaks. Gently fold in the chopped nuts.

3 Divide the reserved apricot mixture between four dessert glasses. Spoon over the cream mixture and chill in the refrigerator for 3–4 hours.

4 Decorate each dessert with edible silver or gold leaf, if using, and serve immediately.

TIP

To use the silver or gold leaf, put the shiny side on the dessert, with the paper backing facing up, and use a paintbrush to dab on the paper side. The silver will transfer to the dessert.

Kheer

RICE PUDDING WITH CARDAMOM & PISTACHIOS

This rich, creamy dessert from northern India can be made to be thick or very liquid with the rice floating in the milk, depending on your personal preference. This lightly spiced version is delicious served with fresh fruit.

SERVES: 4–6

85 g/3 oz basmati rice

1.2 litres/2 pints full-fat milk, plus extra to taste

seeds from 4 green cardamom pods

1 cinnamon stick

100 g/3½ oz caster sugar, or to taste

TO SERVE

grated palm sugar or soft light brown sugar

chopped toasted pistachio nuts

PREP: 5 minutes, plus soaking & chilling time

1 Wash the rice in several changes of water until the water runs clear, then leave to soak in a bowl of fresh cold water for 30 minutes. Drain and set aside until ready to cook.

2 Rinse a saucepan with water and do not dry. Pour the milk into the pan, add the cardamom seeds and cinnamon stick and stir in the rice and caster sugar.

3 Put the pan over a medium–high heat and slowly bring to the boil, stirring. Reduce the heat to its lowest setting and leave the mixture to simmer, stirring frequently, for about 1 hour, until the rice is tender and the mixture has thickened. When the rice is tender, you can stir in extra milk if you like the pudding with a soupier texture, or continue simmering if you like it thicker.

COOK: 1¼–1½ hours

4 Serve hot or transfer to a bowl and leave to cool completely, stirring frequently, then cover and chill. When ready to serve, spoon into individual bowls and sprinkle with the palm sugar and pistachio nuts.

Shrikhand anaari

SAFFRON YOGURT WITH POMEGRANATE

This is the west Indian way of transforming everyday yogurt into a luscious dessert. In Maharashtra, *shrikhand* is traditionally served with hot pooris, straight from the pan, but fresh fruit also makes a tasty accompaniment.

SERVES: 4

PREP: 10–15 minutes, plus draining & chilling

COOK: 5 minutes, plus infusing time

1 kg/2 lb 4 oz wholemilk natural yogurt
¼ tsp saffron threads
2 tbsp full-fat milk
55 g/2 oz caster sugar, or to taste
seeds from 2 green cardamom pods
2 pomegranates

1 Line a sieve set over a bowl with a piece of muslin large enough to hang over the edges. Add the yogurt, then tie the corners of the muslin into a tight knot and tie them to a kitchen tap. Allow the bundle to hang over the sink for 4 hours, or until the excess moisture has dripped away.

2 Put the saffron threads in a dry pan over a high heat and toast, stirring frequently, until you can smell the aroma. Immediately tip them out of the pan.

3 Put the milk in the pan, return the saffron threads and warm until bubbles appear around the edge, then set aside and leave to infuse.

4 When the yogurt is thick and creamy, put it in a bowl, stir in the sugar, cardamom seeds and the saffron and milk mixture and beat until smooth. Taste and add extra sugar, if desired. Cover and chill for at least 1 hour, until well chilled.

5 Meanwhile, to prepare the pomegranates, cut each in half and use your fingers to scoop out the seeds.

6 To serve, spoon the yogurt mixture into individual bowls and sprinkle over the pomegranate seeds.

TIP

For an everyday family dessert, omit the saffron threads and cardamom seeds. Flavour with ground ginger and cinnamon and add sugar to taste.

Mishti doi

BENGALI CARAMEL YOGURT

Traditionally set in earthenware pots, this sweetened yogurt dish is the quintessential dessert, without which a Bengali meal cannot be complete. You can add a small pinch of saffron threads to flavour the milk mixture, if desired.

SERVES: 4

400 g/14 oz evaporated milk
200 g/7 oz condensed milk
2 tbsp caster sugar
100 g/3½ oz set natural yogurt, whisked

PREP: 5 minutes,
plus chilling time

1 Pour the evaporated milk and condensed milk into a saucepan over a medium heat and bring to the boil. Reduce the heat to low, stir and simmer gently for 10 minutes, or until well combined. Remove from the heat.

2 Meanwhile, in a separate small saucepan, heat the sugar over a low heat until it starts to melt, turns golden and begins to caramelize. Remove from the heat.

COOK: 20 minutes,
plus standing time

3 Add the caramelized sugar to the milk mixture and stir to mix well. When the milk mixture is just warm, stir in the yogurt and mix well.

4 Pour the mixture into four small serving bowls, cover with clingfilm and leave to stand in a warm place for 8–10 hours or overnight, until lightly set. Transfer to the refrigerator and chill for 4–6 hours before serving.

TIP

Add a teaspoon of ground cardamom seeds to the milk mixture for a spicier flavour, if you like.

Bebinca

GOAN LAYERED COCONUT CAKE

This rich Goan dessert has its influence from the Portuguese, who ruled Goa from the 16th century until its liberation in 1961. It is a dense, moist cake that is traditionally cooked layer by layer over hot coals. It is time-consuming to make but the result is well worth the effort. It is delicious served cold with vanilla ice cream.

SERVES: 8–10

PREP: 15 minutes, plus chilling time

COOK: 1¾–2 hours

400 ml/14 fl oz coconut milk

300 g/10½ oz golden caster sugar

10 egg yolks, lightly beaten

200 g/7 oz plain flour

½ tsp freshly grated nutmeg

1 tsp freshly ground cardamom seeds

pinch of ground cloves

¼ tsp ground cinnamon

100 g/3½ oz butter, plus extra for greasing

1 Preheat the oven to 200°C/400°F/ Gas Mark 6. Lightly grease a 17-cm/ 6½-inch non-stick, round cake tin and line with baking paper.

2 Pour the coconut milk into a saucepan and stir in the sugar. Heat gently for 8–10 minutes, stirring until the sugar has dissolved. Remove from the heat and gradually add the beaten egg yolks, whisking all the time so that the eggs do not scramble and the mixture is smooth. Sift in the flour and spices and stir to make a smooth batter.

3 Melt the butter, then add a tablespoon to the prepared tin and spread over the base. Pour an eighth of the batter into the tin and spread to coat the base evenly. Bake in the preheated oven for 10–12 minutes, or until set.

4 Remove from the oven and brush another spoonful of the melted butter over the top, followed by another eighth of the batter. Return to the oven and cook for 10–12 minutes, or until set.

5 Repeat this process until all the butter and batter has been used up, baking for a further 20–25 minutes, or until the top is golden brown and the cake is firmly set. Remove from the oven and allow to cool in the tin.

6 When cool, remove the cake from the tin, cover with clingfilm and chill for 4–6 hours before serving.

Masala chai

MASALA TEA

There is always time for a cup of tea, or *chai*. Many offices in India have a *chai walla*, and vendors sell it freshly brewed on street corners and train platforms. This milky version is drunk all over India.

SERVES: 4

PREP: 5 minutes

COOK: 15 minutes, plus infusing time

1 litre/1¾ pints cold water

2.5-cm/1-inch piece fresh ginger, roughly chopped

1 cinnamon stick

3 green cardamom pods, crushed

3 cloves

1½ tbsp Assam tea leaves

sugar and milk, to taste

1 Pour the water into a heavy-based saucepan over a medium–high heat. Add the ginger, cinnamon stick, cardamom pods and cloves and bring to the boil. Reduce the heat and simmer for 10 minutes.

2 Put the tea leaves in a teapot and pour over the water and spices. Stir and leave to infuse for 5 minutes.

3 Strain the tea into four teacups or heatproof glasses and add sugar and milk to taste.

TIP

For iced masala tea, allow the tea to cool completely in step 2, then strain into a jug and chill. Serve in tall glasses with ice, sugar and lemon wedges.

Namkeen lassi

SALT LASSI

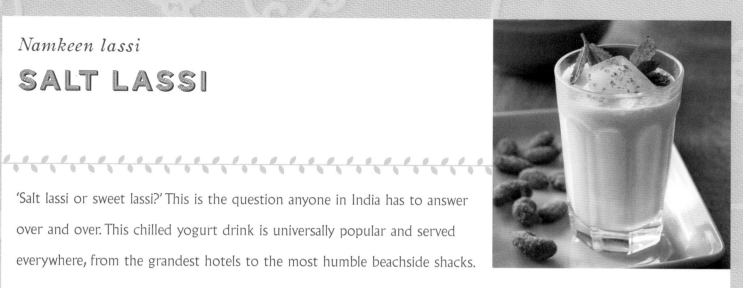

'Salt lassi or sweet lassi?' This is the question anyone in India has to answer over and over. This chilled yogurt drink is universally popular and served everywhere, from the grandest hotels to the most humble beachside shacks.

SERVES: 4

PREP: 5 minutes

COOK: 0 minutes

700 g/1 lb 9 oz wholemilk natural yogurt

½ tsp salt

¼ tsp sugar

250 ml/9 fl oz cold water

ice cubes, to serve

ground cumin and fresh mint sprigs, to decorate

1 Beat together the yogurt, salt and sugar in a jug or bowl, then add the water and whisk until frothy.

2 Fill four glasses with ice cubes and pour over the yogurt mixture. Lightly dust with cumin and top with mint sprigs to decorate.

TIP

For a sweet lassi, add 4 tablespoons of sugar and omit the salt. Decorate with ground cumin and very finely chopped toasted pistachios.

Falooda
ROSE & VERMICELLI MILKSHAKE

Falooda is popular not just in Mumbai, where it is thought to have originated, but also in the rest of the country. This chilled drink/dessert is the perfect way to cool off in the summer heat. *Tukmaria* or basil seeds, used in this recipe, have a very mild flavour (rather like poppy seeds) and are generally used in light desserts.

SERVES: 4

PREP: 20 minutes, plus soaking time

COOK: 5–10 minutes

2 tsp edible basil seeds (tukmaria)
200 ml/7 fl oz cold water
10 g/¼ oz very fine rice vermicelli (sevai)
125 ml/4 fl oz rose syrup
1 litre/1¾ pints chilled milk
4 scoops of vanilla ice cream

1 Place the basil seeds in a bowl and pour over the water. Leave to soak for 15 minutes, or until swollen and jelly-like. Drain and set aside.

2 Meanwhile, break the vermicelli into small pieces and cook according to the packet instructions. Drain and refresh under cold running water.

3 To assemble the drinks, pour the rose syrup into the bases of four glasses. Divide the soaked basil seeds and the drained vermicelli between the glasses.

4 Pour over the chilled milk and top each with a scoop of ice cream. Serve immediately.

TIP
For a mango falooda, replace the rose syrup with mango purée.